The Gospel in
The
Feasts
of
Israel

The Gospel in
The Feasts of Israel

by

VICTOR BUKSBAZEN

CHRISTIAN • LITERATURE • CRUSADE
Fort Washington, Pennsylvania 19034

CHRISTIAN LITERATURE CRUSADE

U.S.A.
P.O. Box 1449, Fort Washington, PA 19034

Copyright © 1954
The Friends of Israel
Gospel Ministry, Inc.
Bellmawr, NJ 08099

This edition, edited and reset 1992
Under special arrangements with
The Friends of Israel Gospel Ministry
This printing 1996

ISBN 0-87508-043-X

PRINTED IN THE UNITED STATES OF AMERICA

FOREWORD

BY OSWALD J. SMITH, LITT.D.

As I read *The Gospel in the Feasts of Israel,* I was amazed at the author's depth of understanding and the evidence of his penetrating study and spiritual insight. Here we have a true masterpiece that should be read with real profit by all—Jews and Gentiles alike.

Mr. Buksbazen throws an abundance of new light on a number of very difficult problems and draws on his background of learning in the Holy Scriptures and Jewish lore to bring out precious truths not always discernible at first sight.

His explanation of the customs, practices, and beliefs of the Jewish people is most illuminating and instructive, and his interpretation of Hebrew terms is clear and convincing. The author's presentation of the various feasts of Israel will prove helpful to every student of the Word of God and every Christian worker.

It has been my privilege to know Mr. Buksbazen for a number of years now, and I think of him first as a missionary, then as a Christian gentleman, and now as an expositor and author.

Many will undoubtedly study *The Gospel in the Feasts of Israel* with deep interest, and some, I trust, will be brought to the Savior as a result, for no one can read it without being moved Godward.

I heartily commend it and pray that it will enjoy a widespread distribution, not only in America but throughout the entire world.

Oswald J. Smith,
The People's Church
Toronto, Ontario, Canada

CONTENTS

ILLUSTRATIONS

Booths of Branches on the Housetops

CHAPTER ONE

PASSOVER AND
THE LORD'S SUPPER

Beneath the blood-stained lintel I with my
children stand;
A messenger of evil is passing through the
land.
There is no other refuge from the destroyer's
face;
Beneath the blood-stained lintel shall be our
hiding place.

The Lamb of God has suffered, our sins and
griefs He bore;
By faith the blood is sprinkled above our
dwelling's door.
The foe who seeks to enter doth fear that
sacred sign;
Tonight the blood-stained lintel shall shelter
me and mine.

JUDAISM and Christianity are as insepa-
rable as seed and flower, or tree and fruit.
Nowhere can the organic relationship between
the two be observed more clearly than in the
Passover of the Jews and the Last Supper as
ordained by our Lord, when He and His twelve
disciples sat around the Passover table.

Now on the first day of the feast of unleavened bread, the disciples came to Jesus, saying unto him, Where wilt thou that we prepare for thee to eat the passover? And he said, Go into the city to such a man, and say unto him, The Master saith, My time is at hand; I will keep the passover at thy house with my disciples. And the disciples did as Jesus had appointed them, and they made ready the passover (Matthew 26:17–19).

In the light of the New Testament we obtain a full understanding of the Passover, while the deepest meaning of the Lord's Supper cannot be fathomed without the historic background of the Jewish Passover.

Did the Jews in the time of our Lord celebrate the Passover the same way as they do today? Substantially yes, for the Jews preserve their traditions tenaciously and faithfully.

Passover and Easter Related

Passover and Easter generally coincide in time (usually March or early April). There is, however, a deeper spiritual interdependence and unity between them. Wherever there is a city with a major Jewish population, you will observe feverish preparations for the Passover—a joyful and solemn occasion, officially designated the "Season of Liberation" and also the "Season of Joy."

The deliverance of Israel from Egypt is the

central point in Jewish history and worship, even as Calvary is the central point in the Christian faith. On Calvary the work of redemption was accomplished for every believer.

Passover Preparations

On the eve before the day of Passover, Jewish homes are cleansed of all leaven, in accordance with the command of the Lord in Exo-

BAKING OF MATZOS (UNLEAVENED BREAD)

dus 12:15: "Seven days shall ye eat unleavened bread; even the first day ye shall put away leaven out of your houses; for whosoever eateth leavened bread from the first day until the seventh day, that soul shall be cut off from Israel."

Most likely the youngest son helps father perform the *mitzva* (a meritorious deed). Obligingly, the little boy scatters a few crumbs in the corners of the house so that father may sweep them away and pronounce the traditional benediction for the occasion: "Blessed art thou, Lord our God, King of the universe, who has sanctified us with thy commandments and commanded us to remove all leaven from our household."

For days and weeks mother is busy giving the house a thorough spring cleaning in preparation for that great season of *Pesach*, the Passover. Also the pots and pans must be cleansed in boiling water to remove all vestige of leaven that might possibly cling to them, before they can be used for the feast of the "Unleavened Bread."

Only then can the *matzos*, the unleav-ened bread, be brought into the home.

In the evening, after the service in the synagogue, father returns to a festively decorated home. The family, dressed in holiday finery, is assembled around the table. Now father is ready to preside, reclining in kingly manner, and conduct the celebration. The traditional symbols of the Passover are spread on the table. The house is well lit even as were the Hebrew homes when darkness descended in Egypt.

Elijah—Messiah's Herald

A place of honor is reserved for Elijah, the herald of the Messiah, in the hope that he will come on this most solemn night and announce the joyful news that Messiah has at last come, for the rabbis say that Messiah is most likely to come on the night of Passover. And so a place at the table is set for Elijah, the traditional cup of Elijah is filled, and an empty chair awaits the heavenly guest. Will he come? Will he sip the wine? These are the secret questions of every heart, especially of the still hopeful and trusting younger generation. What high hopes that cup symbolizes, and what dreams are shattered at the sight of its remaining untouched!

Passover Symbols

We observe on the Passover table a glass of salt water, symbolic of the Red Sea through which God led His people and also reminiscent of the tears the Hebrew ancestors shed during their enslavement.

Also, three pieces of unleavened bread, or matzos, are covered with a white napkin. These matzos are descendants in a straight line from the original unleavened cakes that the Jews hastily prepared when the truculent Pharaoh at last decreed that the Jews leave Egypt—immediately.

Prominent among the Passover symbols is the shank bone in place of the lamb that God commanded be eaten in every Jewish household on the night of the Passover. "In the tenth day of this month they shall take to them every man a lamb, according to the house of their fathers, a lamb for an house" (Exodus 12:3).

This is the eternal reminder that it was the blood of the lamb, sprinkled on the doorposts of every Jewish home, which stood between them and death on that Passover night when God caused His wrath to fall on the firstborn of Egypt.

The four cups of red wine are symbols of the blood of the lamb, and the hard-boiled egg is symbolic of the second sacrifice for the Passover day. The bitter herbs, usually horseradish, bring tears to the eyes of the participants and remind them of the bitterness and sorrow of the former slaves of Pharaoh, their own forefathers.

The *charoseth* is a claylike substance made of apples and nuts, which typifies the clay from which the Israelites were forced to fashion bricks to build the mighty cities and fortresses of the Pharaohs, Pithom and Raamses.

It was probably at this point that our Savior washed His hands, girded Himself with a towel, and stooped to wash the feet of the disciples. "He . . . took a towel, and girded himself . . . and began to wash the disciples' feet" (John 13:4–5).

We Were Slaves in Egypt

And now the father washes his hands and pronounces the benediction over the wine, and all drink of it, even as our Lord and His disciples did.

Then begins the long recital, in a sonorous chanting voice, of the story of God's deliverance of His people from Egypt: "We were slaves of Pharaoh in Egypt. . . ."

For two hours he relates in detail the events preceding Passover, enlarging on every point, for it is a good and meritorious deed to make much of God's mighty exploits. At one point all the symbols on the table are explained. The poor and hungry are invited to come in and partake.

When counting the ten plagues that God sent on Pharaoh and his people, the father dips his finger in the cup, causing one drop of wine to fall for each plague, and counts: *Daam, tsefardea, kinim*—blood, frogs, vermin. . . .

Only one thing, the essence of the Passover, is missing—the lamb, ordained to be sacrificed and consumed by every Jewish family. Passover without the lamb is like a wedding without the bride. What the modern Jews celebrate today is not the Passover but the

Feast of Unleavened Bread.

Nevertheless, the people rejoice, remembering what God did for their ancestors in delivering them from slavery, making them a new people under God, and bringing them into the Promised Land.

Year after year, for some thirty-five centuries, the Jews have repeated the story with unfailing regularity, witnessing for God to the nations of the world, drawing renewed hope and strength to carry them through whatever suffering and persecution the rolling years may bring their way. He who delivered His people from Pharaoh, Haman, Hitler, and Stalin will not fail His people, whatever betide.

Passover is the story of deliverance, a harbinger of a greater redemption yet to come, the vehicle of the undying Messianic hope.

The Last Passover in the Upper Room

During a recent visit to the land of Israel, I stood on Mount Zion, overlooking the ancient city of Jerusalem, with Gethsemane, Calvary, and the Mount of Olives on the near horizon. Close by is an ancient house with one room called the "Coenaculum." This is the Upper Room where the Lord Jesus Christ and His twelve disciples ate their Passover meal and where Jesus ordained the most sacred rite among Christians, the Lord's Supper, commemorating His death, resurrection, and coming again.

It was in this Upper Room that Passover at

last obtained its real meaning and deepest significance.

Let us consider that great event when the Lord and His twelve disciples gathered together in this room to eat the Passover. His heart yearned to be with His nearest family, the twelve. "With desire I have desired to eat this passover with you before I suffer" (Luke 22:15).

They sat together and observed the Passover as ordered by God in Exodus 12. But new life was now infused into this ancient observance by the one who was the final reality of the Passover story.

Now the full significance of Israel's deliverance from Egypt was at last unfolded. Here

"Seven days shall ye eat unleavened bread"
—Exodus 12:15

HAPPY YEMENITE WOMAN CARRYING SUPPLY OF
UNLEAVENED BREAD FOR PASSOVER

was "the Lamb of God" in the person of the Messiah Himself, about to shed His blood on the cross, that all who would believe in Him might be set free from the Egypt of sin and darkness and enabled to begin a new life as children of God.

Among the many symbolic actions of the Passover, there is the eating of the *afikomen*. Early in the meal the father takes the middle matzo of the three unleavened cakes, breaks it, and, after pronouncing a benediction, distributes half among the members of the family, then hides the second half to be brought forth at the end of the meal.

In like manner, the Lord Jesus Christ sat down with His disciples and took the bread, blessed it, broke it, and divided it among His disciples, saying, "Take, eat; this is my body, which is broken for you: this do in remembrance of me" (1 Corinthians 11:24).

How strange that the hidden half of the unleavened middle cake should be preserved as a symbol and rite even to the present day— a wonderful testimony to the broken body of the Lord Jesus Christ and His resurrection. Strange and beyond explanation are the wonderful ways of our God.

The red wine on the Passover table brings to memory the blood of the lamb through which the Children of Israel were saved from death. Our Savior, too, drank of that red wine, after blessing it and dividing it among His disciples, saying, "This cup is the new testament in my blood: this do, as often as ye drink it, in remembrance of me" (1 Corinthians 11:25).

Jesus Himself was the final reality of what the Passover lamb was originally intended to convey. It is His blood that saves Jew and Gentile alike from the death of sin and eternal condemnation and makes the believer a child of God.

The Hymn the Lord Sang

At the end of the Passover celebration, the *Hallel* (Psalms 113—118) is sung. In Psalm 118:21–24 we find the words:

> I will praise thee; for thou hast heard me, and art become my salvation.
>
> The stone which the builders refused is become the head of the corner.
>
> This is the LORD's doing; it is marvelous in our eyes.
>
> This is the day which the Lord hath made; we will rejoice and be glad in it.

These were the very words that our Lord and His disciples sang after the Passover feast. As we read: "And when they had sung an hymn, they went out into the Mount of Olives" (Matthew 26:30).

In the mouth of our Lord the words of the psalm take on a remarkable significance. He Himself was the stone which the builders rejected and the cornerstone of God's mighty edifice, His kingdom. Christ is the foundation and cornerstone, the Alpha and Omega, the sanctuary of God in whom men of all generations and every race have found refuge and peace for their souls. "This is the Lord's doing," and indeed "it is marvelous in our eyes."

And so the Passover and the Lord's Supper merge into one complete story of deliverance and salvation. Every time a Jew partakes of the Passover, he unconsciously bears witness to the Messiah. Every time a Christian partakes of the Lord's Supper, he remembers Him of whom the Passover lamb was a portrayal, the Messiah who died for him and by whose blood he is cleansed and forgiven.

Christ Arose—as David Foretold

The story of the Passover and the Lord's Supper would be incomplete without the resurrection of our Lord. The account of Jesus' life does not end with His death on the cross and burial in a borrowed tomb. If this were the end, the cross would signify a beautiful but tragic life. But Christ arose victorious over death, raised up by the power of God, according to His Word that He would not permit His Holy One to see corruption (Psalm 16:10).

Christ arose, the firstfruits of resurrection, bringing to all believers the assurance that if we die in Him, we shall also live through Him and with Him: "But now is Christ risen from the dead and become the firstfruits of them that slept. For since by man came death, by man came also the resurrection of the dead. For as in Adam all die, even so in Christ shall all be made alive" (1 Corinthians 15:20–22).

Today on Mount Zion there is a shrine dear to the hearts of Jews throughout the world. It holds the tomb of David, beloved king of the Jews, upon which, engraved in golden Hebrew letters, are the words, "David the King of Israel lives for evermore."

I am sure the Apostle Peter must have known this tomb for he spoke about it quite clearly in the Acts of the Apostles when, on the day of Pentecost, he addressed a large number of Jews in Jerusalem, saying:

Men and brethren, let me freely speak unto you of the patriarch, David, that he is

TOMB OF DAVID ON MOUNT ZION

"Men and brethren, let me freely speak unto you of the patrarch David, that he is both dead and buried, and his sepulchre is with us unto this day"— Acts 2:29

both dead and buried, and his sepulchre is with us unto this day. Therefore, being a prophet, and knowing that God had sworn with an oath to him, that of the fruit of his loins, according to the flesh, he would raise up Christ to sit on his throne; he, seeing this before, spoke of the resurrection of Christ, that his soul was not left in hades, neither his flesh did see corruption. This Jesus hath God raised up, whereof we all are witnesses (Acts 2:29–32).

As a result of this sermon, 3,000 souls surrendered in faith to the Messiah. The first Church of Christ, consisting of 3,000 believers, was established in Jerusalem.

Christ Our Passover

The Apostle Paul, writing by the Holy Spirit, summed up the significance of this Passover for every child of God when he wrote, "Christ, our passover, is sacrificed for us. Therefore, let us keep the feast, not with old leaven, neither with the leaven of malice and wickedness, but with the unleavened bread of sincerity and truth" (1 Corinthians 5:7–8).

Contemplating the story of the Passover and the story of the crucifixion and resurrection of the Lord Jesus Christ, the words of the beloved disciple come to mind: "Behold, what manner of love the Father hath bestowed upon us, that we should be called the children of God" (1 John 3:1).

CHAPTER TWO

THE FEAST OF WEEKS— PENTECOST

Rite and Reality

THREE times a year the Israelites were commanded to appear before God in the holy Temple in Jerusalem. The occasions were the Passover (celebrating deliverance from Egypt and symbolized by the eating of the unleavened bread and the offering of the Passover lamb), Pentecost (the Feast of Weeks, typified by the offering of two wave loaves made of newly harvested wheat), and the Feast of Tabernacles (symbolized by the booths commemorating Israel's wandering through the wilderness and final entrance into the land of promise) (Deuteronomy 16:16).

The word *Pentecost* is Greek, meaning "fifty." It was so designated because it was observed on the fiftieth day after the Passover Sabbath. These are the words of the institution of Pentecost in the Old Testament:

> And ye shall count unto you from the next day after the sabbath, from the day

that ye brought the sheaf of the wave offering; seven sabbaths shall be complete: even unto the next day after the seventh sabbath shall ye number fifty days; and ye shall offer a new meal offering unto the LORD. Ye shall bring out of your habitations *two wave loaves* of two tenth parts; they shall be of fine flour; they shall be *baked with leaven*; they are the first fruits unto the LORD (Leviticus 23:15–17).

In Exodus 34:22, it is briefly described as follows: "And thou shalt observe the *feast of weeks*, of the firstfruits of wheat harvest, and

"The first of the firstfruits of thy land thou shalt bring into the house of the Lord thy God"—
Exodus 23:19

the feast of ingathering at the year's end."

For centuries Israel was an agricultural nation depending on the produce of the land for her sustenance. Pentecost was the feast of the ingathering of the firstfruits of the wheat harvest, a thanksgiving festival in which Israel expressed her dependence on God for harvest and daily bread.

The Feast of Weeks was a most popular holiday, falling in early summer when the cloudless skies of the promised land are blue and benign, the weather caressingly warm and generally unmarred by the scorching desert wind, the *Hamsin.*

From every part of the country Jews would stream to Jerusalem to appear before their God. Also visitors from abroad, from among the diaspora of Israel, would gather for the Feast of Weeks.

In time, when the Jews became dispersed among the nations, Pentecost lost its primary character as a harvest festival and became known as "The Feast of the Giving of the Law." Ancient rabbis, by careful calculation and time reckoning, came to the conclusion that God gave the Law to Moses on the day of Pentecost. Hence, Pentecost is also known as "The Season of the Giving of the Law" and is a time of rejoicing among the Jews.

Pentecost—the Birthday of Judaism

Being the anniversary of the giving of the

Law on Mount Sinai, Pentecost is considered as the birthday of Judaism.

In Leviticus 23:11 we read that on the day after the Sabbath (that is, the Passover Sabbath) the priest was to bring the sheaf of the wave offering into the Temple, signifying the beginning of the new harvest, the beginning of the firstfruit.

Strangely, these words were to become prophetic of the one who, on the very day after the Passover Sabbath, would rise from the dead and become the "firstfruits of the resurrection" (1 Corinthians 15:20).

Then on the day of Pentecost "two wave loaves" were brought to the Lord, loaves made of fine flour ground of the new wheat and baked with leaven. Of all the cereal offerings, only the wave loaves were baked with leaven. Why leaven? And why *two* wave loaves? Leaven is symbolic of sin. The Passover bread was unleavened because it signified the sinless body of Christ who, being without sin, became sin for our sakes. But the two wave loaves were symbolic of Israel in whom there is the leaven of sin.

Pentecost—the Birthday of the Church

Fifteen hundred years had passed since God commanded His people, through Moses, to observe the Feast of Weeks. Much had happened in that time. Prophets came and went, all foretelling the coming of a Savior to redeem Israel from sin. At last He who was prophesied, Jesus the Messiah, came. He was crucified, according to the eternal purpose of God. He died to save Israel. Then He rose, according to prophecy, and, before ascending to Heaven, commanded His disciples to wait in Jerusalem until they were endued with the Holy Spirit. They waited forty-nine days after His resurrection, even as the Jews waited forty-nine days from Passover to Pentecost.

And when the day of Pentecost was fully come, they were all with one accord in one place. And suddenly there came a sound from heaven like a rushing mighty wind, and it filled all the house where they were sitting. . . . And there were dwelling at Jerusalem Jews, devout men, out of every nation under heaven (Acts 2:1–2, 5).

On this day of Pentecost, Peter addressed his countrymen from every part of the world who had come to Jerusalem, as well as a number of Gentile proselytes, witnessing to them concerning Christ and ending with this exhortation: "Save yourselves from this crooked generation" (v. 40).

And the power of the Holy Spirit worked so mightily in Peter that we read, "Then they that gladly received his word were baptized; and the same day there were added unto them about three thousand souls. And they continued stedfastly in the apostles' doctrine and fellowship, and in breaking of bread, and in prayers" (Acts 2:41–42).

Thus the Church of Christ, made up of 3,000 Jews and some Gentile proselytes, was born.

Now we are beginning to see the meaning of the *two* wave loaves baked with leaven. The Church of Christ, of which both Jew and Gentile are members, is not without sin. It contains leaven, the symbol of sin, reminding us to look for perfection *not* in the Church but in *Him*, the perfect Son of God, in whom there is no leaven of sin.

The 3,000 Jewish believers were the spiritual firstfruits of the Church of Christ. Thus, the Old Testament symbol, the two wave loaves, became a glorious reality in the New— a Church composed of Jewish and Gentile believers purchased by the blood of the Lamb.

Ruth the Ancestress of Jesus

On the day of Pentecost the Jews, even to the present day, read the Book of Ruth. They do this for two reasons. First, because the Book of Ruth has a rustic setting—Bethlehem at harvest time. Thus, it is preeminently suitable for a harvest festival. Second, it presents Ruth the Moabitess, a Gentile woman, who came to know and love the God of Naomi, the Jewess. Here hope and prophecy combine. They look to the day when Jew and Gentile will worship God together through the Kinsman-Redeemer, Christ, typified by Boaz, the friend and husband of Ruth, his Gentile bride.

In Ruth we have a gracious story of love, faithfulness, and friendship stronger than death, a story unmatched and unsur-passed in all the literature of the world.

Listen to the grief-sticken widow, Naomi, as she speaks to her Gentile daughters-in-law, who lost their husbands, her sons, through famine:

> And Naomi said unto her two daughters-in-law, Go, return each to her mother's house; the LORD deal kindly with you, as ye have dealt with the dead, and with me. The LORD grant you that ye may find rest, each

RUTH AND BOAZ

of you in the house of her husband. Then she kissed them; and they lifted up their voice, and wept (Ruth 1:8–9).

Orpah allowed herself to be persuaded to leave her mother-in-law, but Ruth clave to her. Then Naomi spoke again:

> Behold, thy sister-in-law is gone back unto her people, and unto her gods; return thou after thy sister-in-law. And Ruth said, Entreat me not to leave thee, or to turn away from following after thee; for where thou goest, I will go; and where thou lodgest, I will lodge: *thy people shall be my people, and thy God, my God.* Where thou diest, will I die, and there will I be buried; the LORD do so to me, and more also, if anything but death part thee and me. When she saw that she was stedfastly determined to go with her, then she ceased speaking unto her (Ruth 1:15–18).

Lovely Ruth, the Gentile woman of Moab, came to be not only a child of the God of Abraham, Isaac, and Jacob but an ancestress of King David and his greater Son, Jesus the Messiah (Matthew 1:1–16).

The Spiritual Commonwealth of Israel

Pentecost of the old Jewish dispensation was pointing to the time when Jew and Gentile would come to know and worship the one holy God of Israel. In Christ alone this vision becomes a reality. Today saved Jews and Gentiles are united in one Church, of which the Lord Jesus Christ is both the cornerstone and head.

The Apostle Paul, writing to the Ephe-sians, spoke of this Church of Christ as the spiritual commonwealth of Israel, describing it in this way:

Wherefore, remember that ye, being in time past Gentiles in the flesh, who are called Uncircumcision by that which is called the Circumcision in the flesh made by hands—that at that time ye were without Christ, being aliens from the commonwealth of Israel, and strangers from the covenants of promise, having no hope, and without God in the world. But now in Christ Jesus ye who once were far off are made near by the blood of Christ. . . . Now, therefore, ye are no more strangers and sojourners, but fellow citizens with the saints, and of the household of God; and are built upon the foundation of the apostles and prophets, Jesus Christ himself being the chief corner stone, in whom all the building fitly framed together groweth unto an holy temple in the Lord; in whom ye also are built together for an habitation of God through the Spirit (Ephesians 2:11–13, 19–22).

The Mute Shall Speak Again

On the day of Pentecost the apostles, being filled with the Holy Spirit, spoke in a multitude of tongues, witnessing for the Lord. Even today the apostles of the Lord Jesus Christ, filled with His Spirit and love, go out to every nation and tongue and bring the gospel of salvation in over 1,000 tongues and dialects, not counting the cost, holding everything they have as dung for the sake of Christ their Savior.

But Israel is still the mute servant of the Lord. Endowed with the gift of tongues as no other people, they still are mute as far as the carrying of the gospel to the nations of the world is concerned.

It is significant and enlightening that those children of Israel who have accepted the Lord Jesus Christ as their Messiah and Savior have gone out to the nations with the word of life and light. Their number is legion, for God has not left Himself without a witness among His people Israel, even from the first Jewish apostles of the Messiah Jesus to our present generation. When He comes to make up His jewels, their names shall shine bright as the stars.

Oh, that the day may come when the Lord will loosen the tongues of His servant Israel, and they will go out to witness for Him in every part of the earth, all their talents and gifts quickened and energized by the working of the Spirit of God in them.

CHAPTER THREE

ROSH HASHANA—THE NEW YEAR

A CTUALLY there are two New Years in Judaism. One, according to Biblical time reckoning, begins on the first day of the month of Nisan or Abib, which means "Spring." This month is roughly equivalent to our April. "And the LORD spoke unto Moses and Aaron in the land of Egypt, saying, This month shall be unto you the beginning of months: it shall be the first month of the year to you" (Exodus 12:1–2).

The other New Year's Day, *Rosh Hashana* (literally "Head of the Year"), which the Jews officially recognize and celebrate, is the first day of the seventh month, Tishri, according to the Jewish calendar.

In Leviticus 23:24 we read, "In the seventh month, in the first day of the month, shall ye have *a sabbath, a memorial of blowing of trumpets, an holy convocation.*"

The ancient rabbis believed that the Lord created the world in the first week of the month of Tishri. Therefore, the first day of the seventh month is considered the beginning of creation and the beginning of the year; hence the present Jewish time reckoning. As it is generally known, the Jewish year is a lunar year, which is shorter than the solar year by ten days and twenty-one hours. The year is divided into twelve lunar months of 28 or 29 days each. To equalize the difference between the lunar and solar year, about every three years an extra month is added after the twelfth month, or March. This thirteen-month year is the Jewish leap year.

The Sabbatical Month

Tishri, being the seventh month of the year, is a sabbatical month. What the seventh day is to the week, Tishri, the seventh month, is to the year. Hence, the first day is celebrated as

BLOWING OF THE RAM'S HORN

a sabbath, a day of rest and a memorial calling for the blowing of trumpets, with a holy convocation.

In Nehemiah 8:1–12 we read that after Israel returned from the Babylonian captivity, they began again to observe the New Year's Day solemnly. And when the Law was read to them after long neglect, they were so overwhelmed that they broke down and cried and repented until Ezra, their leader, had to comfort them and remind them that it was also a day of rejoicing and thanksgiving to the Lord and that they were to go home comforted and eat.

The Blowing of the Ram's Horn and Its Significance

According to the rabbis, the blowing of the horns and trumpets ordained by the Lord and observed in the Temple in Jerusalem and throughout the land of Israel had a threefold purpose.

First, the trumpet sound called to repentance. It was as a call to the dead to arise and live again, to awaken from sin to regeneration through repentance.

Second, it reminded the Lord that He was in covenant relationship with His people Israel and must deal gently with them, not according to their merits but according to His gracious promises made to Abraham and the patriarchs of old.

Third, it was to confound and to confuse

Satan, who, the rabbis thought, had a special predilection of accusing Israel on New Year's Day, bringing before the Lord all their shortcomings and sins.

The horn used on the solemn occasion of New Year's Day was a ram's horn (*shofar*), bringing to memory Abraham's sacrifice of his son Isaac at the Lord's command. This sacrifice was considered as if accomplished because of Abraham's absolute faith and willingness to do the Lord's bidding, but which God, in His mercy, refrained from exacting, substituting a ram in the place of Isaac.

The Sacrifice of Isaac and the Sacrifice of the Son of God

The Jews make much of Abraham's sacrifice of his son Isaac, referring to it again and again in their prayers, reminding God of Abraham and his faith, which made him willing to sacrifice Isaac. Abraham's sacrifice of Isaac gloriously typified the sacrifice of our Heavenly Father of His Son, the Lord Jesus Christ, and the willingness of the Son to offer Himself for the salvation of all men. Isaac is a beautiful type of Christ.

In Genesis 22:6 we read, ". . . and they went both of them together." Jesus said, "I and my Father are one" (John 10:30). "I do always those things that please him" (John 8:29).

Divine Bookkeeping

New Year's Day is a solemn time of repentance and preparation for the Day of Atonement, which follows ten days after. The rabbis believe that during New Year, which lasts two days, the Lord opens three books. In one book the righteous are registered; in the second are those who are neither wholly righteous nor utterly wicked; and in the third, the wicked are recorded.

The righteous are judged on New Year's Day and receive rewards such as life, welfare, prosperity, security from all manner of evil and harm, and peace.

In the Prayer Book of the Synagogue for the day of New Year, we read the following prayer: "In the book of life, blessing, peace and good sustenance may we be remembered and inscribed before thee, we and all thy people, the house of Israel, for a happy life and peace. Blessed art thou, O Lord, who makest peace."

The Ten Days of Repentance

The second book records the deeds, good and bad, of the intermediate group, those who are not wholly sinful nor altogether righteous. They are given ten days of repentance which are called *Yomim Noraim*, which means the fearsome or awesome days. During that period, depending on the sincerity of their repentance, the Lord will judge them on the Day of Atonement either for life or destruction, riches or poverty, health or hurt.

The wicked and unrepentant can expect only condemnation and death. Since, according to popular Jewish belief, the majority of mankind are neither utterly good nor utterly wicked, the ten days are of the utmost importance. Much therefore depends on the behavior and repentance of the Jew during these "Ten Awesome Days." During that period old enemies seek to make up their differences, charity is given to the poor, and long confessions of sins are repeated in the synagogue prayers.

A New Year's Litany

The following is a typical although incomplete litany, which Jews recite in Hebrew in the synagogue on New Year's Day.

> Our Father, our King, we have sinned before thee.
>
> Our Father, our King, we have no king beside thee.
>
> Our Father, our King, renew unto us a happy year.
>
> Our Father, our King, annul every severe decree concerning us.
>
> Our Father, our King, annul the designs of those who hate us.
>
> Our Father, our King, frustrate the counsel of our enemies.
>
> Our Father, our King, stay the mouths of

our adversaries and of those who accuse us.

Our Father, our King, remove pestilence, sword, famine, captivity and destruction from the children of thy covenant.

Our Father, our King, hold back the plague from thine heritage.

Our Father, our King, forgive and pardon all our iniquities.

Our Father, our King, blot out, and cause our transgressions and sins to pass away before thine eyes.

Our Father, our King, efface in thine abundant mercy all records of our guilt.

Our Father, our King, cause us to return unto thee in perfect repentance.

Our Father, our King, send perfect healing to the sick of thy people.

PRAYER IN A TEL AVIV SYNAGOGUE

Our Father, our King, repeal the evil sentcnce of our judgment.

Our Father, our King, remember us in the book of happy life.

Our Father, our King, inscribe us in the book of redemption and salvation.

Our Father, our King, inscribe us in the book of sustenance and maintenance.

Our Father, our King, inscribe us in the book of merit.

Our Father, our King, inscribe us in the book of forgiveness and pardon.

Our Father, our King, cause salvation to spring forth for us.

Our Father, our King, exalt the horn of Israel thy people.

Our Father, our King, exalt the horn of thy Messiah.

The Glory That Departed

In ancient days, when the Temple existed, special sacrifices were offered consisting of two young bullocks, one ram, and seven lambs of the first year without spot (Numbers 28:11–15). At the offering of these sacrifices over a hundred priests officiated, and the trumpets and shofar were blown.

But these sacrifices, like all the Temple details, were merely a forecast of the perfect sacrifice fulfilled in the person of the Lord Jesus Christ. We who have been washed and redeemed by His blood are eternally grateful that we have been bought with a great price. Although "it is not possible that the blood of bulls and of goats should take away sins" (Hebrews 10:4), His blood avails forevermore.

New Year's Call to Repentance

Prophetically, New Year marks a further stage in God's plan of salvation for Israel first, and then for all of mankind. Passover was the beginning of redemption purchased through the blood of the Lamb, foreshadowing the Lord Jesus Christ, "the Lamb of God, who taketh away the sin of the world" (John 1:29).

Pentecost, the Feast of Firstfruits, is the birthday of Judaism and also signifies the birth of the Church of Christ. This is followed by a long period between the solemn holy days of Pentecost and New Year's Day, typifying Israel's long period of estrangement from God and life in exile.

Then comes the Feast of New Year, presenting a call to repentance and an opportunity to be reconciled with God on the Day of Atonement, which follows ten days after New Year's Day. Then comes the Feast of Tabernacles and Harvest, symbolic of the completion of the Church of God through the final ingathering of those who are to be saved, Jew and Gentile alike, into the body of Christ.

The Apostle Paul was well acquainted with all the Jewish feasts and with all the rites, hopes, and prophetic implications inherent in them. Was he thinking of Rosh Hashana and the blowing of ram's horns, the bugle call to repentance, when he cried out, "Wherefore, he saith, Awake thou that sleepest, and arise from the dead, and Christ shall give thee light" (Ephesians 5:14)?

CHAPTER FOUR

YOM KIPPUR—
THE DAY OF ATONEMENT

THE Day of Atonement, *Yom Kippur,* begins at sundown at the end of the ninth day of Tishri, the seventh month of the Biblical year. Of all Jewish holy occasions, this is the most solemn—"The Sabbath of Sabbaths." The elaborate ritual for the Day of Atonement, as observed in the Tabernacle and the Temple, is described in Leviticus 16.

Yom Kippur is a solemn fast day. For twenty-four awesome hours from sundown to sundown, Jews the world over—young and old, male and female—assemble in synagogues and places of prayer, to seek atonement with God and forgiveness for all their sins. It is "The Day" of judgment and reckoning.

Between New Year's Day and Yom Kippur are ten days which are called "THE TEN DAYS OF REPENTANCE" or "THE AWESOME DAYS." During that period, every Jew searches his heart and seeks to be reconciled with God and his neighbor.

Five days after Yom Kippur comes *Succoth*

or the Feast of Tabernacles, which lasts eight days. Then the cycle of the autumn holidays is concluded with *Simchath Torah*—the Rejoicing over the Law.

Preparation for the Day of Atonement

New Year's Day on the first of Tishri opens the solemn period of repentance preparatory for Yom Kippur. In the afternoon of New Year's Day, Jews throughout the world assemble near rivers, brooks, and oceans to cast away their sins. This ceremony is called *Tashlikh* and is based on Micah 7:19: "He will turn again; he will have compassion upon us; he will subdue our iniquities; and THOU WILT CAST [in Hebrew, *tashlikh*] ALL THEIR SINS INTO THE DEPTHS OF THE SEA."

Wherever Jews honor the traditions of Israel, Tashlikh is observed. In the afternoon of New Year's Day you may see crowds of Jews near larger bodies of water performing the symbolic ritual of "casting away their sins."

Substitutes for the Atoning Sacrifice

Since the Jews have no temple, priest, or sacrifice, substitutes for the atoning sacrifice have been provided by the rabbis. Some of these are repentance, which includes reparation of wrong, prayer, and fasting. Of all the substitutes, repentance, prayer, and charity are considered the most important. Also, a rooster for every male and a hen for each female are used as substitutes for the atoning sacrifice. These sacrifices of hens and roosters are called *Kapporoth*, which means propitiatory or atoning sacrifices. Needless to say, these Kapporoth, or sacrifices of roosters and hens, have no basis in the Word of God but are, rather, the expression of a deep sense of need for atonement through the shedding of blood.

Another substitute for sacrifice is charity. It is significant that the word "charity" in modern Hebrew usage is the same as "righteousness."

One's own sufferings are also considered a substitute, especially the sufferings of the righteous. (Note the striking similarity of this and other rabbinical traditions to Roman Catholicism.)

The Orthodox Jews of Eastern Europe used to observe the custom of inflicting upon themselves thirty-nine stripes called *malkoth*. We recall that the Apostle Paul was, on five occasions, subjected to "forty stripes save one"— an ancient Jewish method of corporal punishment for transgressors.

Another substitute for the sacrifice of atonement, according to the rabbis, is one's own death. The rabbis base this mistaken idea on Psalm 116:15, "Precious in the sight of the LORD is the death of his saints."

The study of the Law, especially of the Talmud, is another substitute.

For a month before the Day of Atonement,

special prayers are offered at midnight for forgiveness. These prayers are known as *Slihoth*—prayers for forgiveness.

In the afternoon preceding the Day of Atonement, a festive meal is consumed by the family in preparation for the ensuing fast. On the Day of Atonement a complete fast is observed, which excludes even the moistening of one's parched lips with water. This fast is to be observed by every Israelite from the age of thirteen upward. Dispensations are granted only to those dangerously ill.

The Day of Atonement services begin at sundown when the cantor, flanked by two members of the congregation and dressed in white garb and headgear, addresses himself to the assembly in the synagogue with this solemn preamble:

> By authority of the Court on high, and by authority of the Court on earth, with the knowledge of the All-Present and with the knowledge of this congregation, we give leave to pray with them that have transgressed.

Kol Nidre—All Vows

After that the cantor begins to intone, in a chanting voice, the most solemn prayer of the Yom Kippur devotions. This is known as *Kol Nidre*—"All Vows." In somber, solemn, chanting tones, he recites:

All vows, bonds, oaths, devotions, promises, penalties, and obligations: wherewith we have vowed, sworn, devoted and bound ourselves: from this Day of Atonement unto the next Day of Atonement, may it come unto us for good: lo, all these, we repent us in them. They shall be absolved, released, annulled, made void, and of none effect: they shall not be binding nor shall they have any power. Our vows shall not be vows: our bonds shall not be bonds: and our oaths shall not be oaths.

This prayer, which the Jews consider as one of the most sacred, has often been criticized as a prayer that absolves all Jews from any form of promise and obligation. But, in fact, the prayer of Kol Nidre merely expresses a deep consciousness of the inability of man to keep in full his vows, promises, bonds, and obligations in relation to God, and that he is always, no matter how conscientious, on the debit side of the ledger. Man can only face his Maker as a suppliant in need of forgiveness.

The Meaning of Yom Kippur

The word Yom Kippur itself, meaning the Day of Atonement, comes from a Hebrew word *kapper*, "to cover." According to this meaning, God covers the sins of His people by the blood of the sacrifice. Thus, God sees only the penalty paid and the person covered with the blood, who appears sinless before Him. This expresses perfectly the idea of substitutionary death and propitiation. It points to the heart of the gospel: "Christ died for our sins" (1 Corinthians 15:3).

Another interpretation of the root of the word *kapper* is *kofer*, which means "a ransom," as in Exodus 21:30: "If there be laid on him a sum of money, then he shall give for the ransom of his life whatsoever is laid upon him." And in 2 Samuel 21:3, when the blood of the murdered Gibeonites cried to heaven for vengeance and David asked, "Wherewith shall I make the atonement?"—the word there is *kapper*. The underlying idea is that there is no atonement except through the blood of the sacrifice. On this all the Jewish commentators are very clear. The Talmud says in Yoma 5a, "There is no atonement except with blood." And in the New Testament, we read in Hebrews 9:22, "Without shedding of blood is no remission."

The Day of Atonement Sacrifices

The appointed sacrifice of the Day of Atonement, according to Scripture (Leviticus 16), is two goats. One of these was the scapegoat (in Hebrew, *azazel*) which carried away all the sins of the Children of Israel into an uninhabited place. "Azazel," therefore, was a type of Christ who was led outside the city walls bearing the sins of His people (Leviticus

16:21–22; Matthew 27:33).

The second goat was killed by the high priest in the Temple, and its blood was sprinkled to make atonement for all the uncleanness and transgressions of the Children of Israel.

In addition to the goats, lambs and bullocks were also sacrificed. An important part in the Day of Atonement ritual was played by the red heifer, which was killed and its blood sprinkled for the cleansing of the people from all defilement of sin (Numbers 19; Hebrews 9:13).

The High Priest as Mediator

The high priest, assisted by over 500 priests, performed the solemn and elaborate rites of Yom Kippur. He was separated for seven days from the people, preparing for this solemn day. On the Day of Atonement the high priest washed his body five times and his hands and his feet ten times.

The climax of the Day of Atonement was when the high priest entered the Most Holy Place where the Ark of the Covenant was placed, with the Mercy Seat overshadowing it. Above it was the Shekinah Glory—the visible presence of God in a cloud.

After killing the bullock and the second goat which had been set apart for Jehovah, he sprinkled the Most Holy Place, the veil, the altar of incense, and the altar of burnt offering, cleansing them from the defilement of sin. He then appeared before the very presence of God, imploring the Lord by His mysterious and sacred name "Jehovah."

The Sacred Tetragrammaton

Only the officiating priests were initiated in the secret of the proper pronunciation of the sacred tetragrammaton YHWH, the holy, mystical, and ineffable name of JEHOVAH. The common people dreaded to use the name of God, for it was instilled into their very fibre, "Thou shalt not take the name of the LORD thy God in vain" (Exodus 20:7). Even today, Orthodox Jews are loath to use the word "Jehovah" in any manner.

It is interesting to note, among the many things of which the Jews accused our Savior (according to the ancient tradition of rabbis) was the alleged fact that the Lord Jesus somehow misappropriated the sacred pronunciation of the name of Jehovah from the high priest and thereby performed miracles. It seems that this was an effort on the part of the rabbis to account for the peculiar relationship between our Lord Jesus and His Heavenly Father, and His position as Mediator between man and God.

While the high priest was in the Most Holy Place in the very presence of God, the people, with mounting tension, waited for his reappearance in dreadful fear that his prolonged time in the Holy of Holies signified that God had not forgiven His people and had slain their unworthy high priest.

When at last the high priest came out of the Most Holy Place, the people sighed with relief that their service had been accepted, their sins forgiven.

Shadow and Reality

A careful study of the Epistle to the Hebrews gives the New Testament believer deeper understanding of the Temple service and its sacrifices, the position of the high priest, and the symbolism of all the rites in their relation to Christ. Without the New Testament, the Old Testament is incomplete, a promise without fulfillment, a shadow without reality. Here we have a divine commentary on the Temple, the high priest, and the sacrifices—all pointing to and speaking of Christ.

But Christ being come an high priest of good things to come, by a greater and more perfect tabernacle, not made with hands, that is to say, not of this building, neither by the blood of goats and calves, but by his own blood he entered in once into the holy place, having obtained eternal redemption for us. For if the blood of bulls and of goats, and the ashes of an heifer sprinkling the unclean, sanctifieth to the purifying of the flesh, how much more shall the blood of Christ, who through the eternal Spirit offered himself without spot to God, purge your conscience from dead works to serve the living God? . . . For when Moses had spoken every precept to all the people according to the law, he took the blood of calves and of goats, with water, and scarlet wool, and hyssop, and sprinkled both the book, and all the people, saying, This is the blood of the testament which God hath enjoined unto you. Moreover, he sprinkled with blood both the tabernacle and all the vessels of the ministry. And almost all things are by the law purged with blood, and without shedding of blood is no remission (Hebrews 9:11–14, 19–22).

It is this Christ who is our Atonement and perfect Mediator with God. In Him all the verities of the Old Testament, the Temple, the high priest, and the sacrifices, have been embodied and fulfilled. "So Christ was once offered to bear the sins of many; and unto them that look for him shall he appear the second time without sin unto salvation" (Hebrews 9:28).

The Mighty Holiness of This Day

Deprived of Temple, priest, and sacrifice, rabbinical Judaism has made a consistent effort to water down the importance of the sacrifices and the shed blood, which alone makes atonement for the soul. In place of the atonements, the Day of Atonement itself has been declared to make atonement for sinners, without the necessity of a sacrifice. This view is reflected in the prayer of Rabbi Amnon of Mayence (circa A.D. 1100). Rabbi Amnon of Mayence is believed to have been a martyr for his Jewish faith. The Archbishop of Mayence urged the rabbi to renounce Judaism and to be baptized. The rabbi steadfastly refused. The exasperated archbishop ordered that the rabbi's hands and feet be mutilated. Dying from his wounds, Rabbi Amnon is said to have composed this prayer in the synagogue on the eve of Yom Kippur.

We will celebrate the mighty holiness of this day, for it is one of awe and terror. Thereon is thy dominion exalted and thy throne is established in mercy, and thou sittest thereon in truth. Verily it is thou alone who art judge and arbiter, who knowest and art witness; thou writest down and settest the seal, thou recordest and tellest; yea, thou rememberest the things forgotten. Thou unfoldest the records, and the deeds therein inscribed proclaim themselves; for lo! the seal of every man's hand is set thereto.

The great trumpet is sounded; the still small voice is heard; the angels are dismayed; fear and trembling seize hold of them as they proclaim, Behold the Day of Judgment! The host of heaven is to be arraigned in judgment. For in thine eyes they are not pure; and all who enter the world dost thou cause to pass before thee as a flock of sheep. As a shepherd seeketh out his flock, and causeth them to pass beneath his crook, so dost thou cause to pass and number, tell and visit every living soul, appointing the measure of every creature's life and decreeing their destiny.

The underlying belief of this prayer is that atonement and forgiveness depend on whether a man's good deeds and merits outweigh his misdeeds and demerits. The basic weakness of Judaism is that it is aware of "sins" but ignores "sin"—the essential bias of man toward evil, the sinfulness of man's very nature.

Inscribed and Sealed

On Yom Kippur God seals the books of accounting that were opened on New Year's Day. Whereas before New Year's Day, Jews wish one another that their name be "inscribed" into the book of life, after New Year's Day and before the Day of Atonement, when greeting one another or sending greetings in writing, the word is "May you be 'sealed' in the book of life."

To the child of God who knows the holiness, righteousness, and purity of God, to have to depend on one's merits or demerits is rather a bleak prospect. King David, one of the most lovely personalities in the Old Testament, deeply conscious of his own sin, cried out, "If thou, LORD, shouldest mark iniquities, O Lord, who shall stand?" (Psalm 130:3).

Messianic Echoes of Yom Kippur

In spite of Yom Kippur, the day dedicated to atonement, there is no assurance of sins forgiven in Judaism. There is longing, there is hope for forgiveness, but there is no assurance. Only the Son of God can give assurance—to those who come to Him in faith. The Day of Atonement is only a substitute for atonement. Judaism could be best summed up as man's attempt to justify himself by his own effort, without the atonement made by a Savior. That cannot be done. There can be no substitute for Christ, our Atonement and Propitiator. Judaism has tried hard to find a substitute for Him. Unscriptural, so-called Christianity, is trying hard even today. The result is only a man-made, substitute religion, which increases the abyss between God and man.

Deep in her heart Israel knows that her atonement is of the Messiah. He alone is able to bring forgiveness. An ancient prayer in the Day of Atonement liturgy, which plainly refers to Isaiah 53, gives witness to this fact in the following plaintive and wistful lines:

Our righteous Messiah has departed from us,

We are horror-stricken, and have none to
justify us.

Our iniquities and the yoke of our transgressions

He carries, who is wounded because of
our transgressions.

He bears on His shoulder the burden of
our sins,

To find pardon for all our iniquities.

By His stripes we shall be healed—

O Eternal One, it is time that Thou
shouldest create Him anew!

Here we clearly see that Judaism is without
true atonement, and there is only a wistful
yearning for it. Judaism still looks to the
Messiah to bring salvation and reconciliation
with God.

The Shofar—the Trump of God

And so the Yom Kippur solemnities are completed by the blowing of the shofar, the ram's
horn—the trumpet that heralds the coming of
the Messiah. Here the hope of Israel and the
hope of the Christian converge. Israel waits
for His First Coming, while the believer in the
Lord Jesus Christ knows that He already came
and saved him. He now looks forward to His
Second Coming when He will establish His
Kingdom on the earth.

For the Lord himself shall descend from
heaven with a shout, with the voice of the

archangel, and with the trump of God; and the dead in Christ shall rise first; then we who are alive and remain shall be caught up together with them in the clouds, to meet the Lord in the air; and so shall we ever be with the Lord (1 Thessalonians 4:16–17).

One day the hope of Israel and the hope of the Church will at last become a reality. The King of Glory will come. But the face of the King will be one—that of the Lord Jesus Christ, the Messiah of Israel, the hope of all nations.

CHAPTER FIVE

SUCCOTH—THE FEAST OF TABERNACLES OR BOOTHS

Also in the fifteenth day of the seventh month, when ye have gathered in the fruit of the land, ye shall keep a feast unto the LORD seven days. On the first day shall be a sabbath, and on the eighth day shall be a sabbath. And ye shall take on the first day the boughs of goodly trees, branches of palm trees, and the boughs of thick trees, and willows of the brook; and ye shall rejoice before the LORD your God seven days. And ye shall keep it a feast unto the LORD seven days in the year. It shall be a statute forever in your generations: ye shall celebrate it in the seventh month. Ye shall dwell in booths seven days; all that are Israelites born shall dwell in booths; that your generations may know that I made the children of Israel to dwell in booths, when I brought them out of the land of Egypt: I am the LORD your God (Leviticus 23:39–43).

An Agricultural and Thanksgiving Festival

THE Feast of Tabernacles comes on the 15th of Tishri, the seventh month according to the Bible calendar. This usually coincides with the end of September or early October.

Jews the world over—from Bombay to Brooklyn, from Jerusalem to San Francisco—are busy erecting booths, according to the prescription the Lord gave to them through Moses in Leviticus 23:33–44.

The Feast of Tabernacles is one of the three great occasions upon which God commanded the Children of Israel to assemble in the Temple at Jerusalem and present their sacrifices and offerings to the Lord. "They shall not appear before the LORD empty" (Deuteronomy 16:16).

The feast is primarily agricultural in character. It is a joyous occasion. The harvest has been brought in from the fields, the groves, and the orchards. Barns and sheds are full. Hearts, too, are full of praise and thanksgiving for God's bounties. It is "The Feast of Ingathering," or Israel's Thanksgiving Festival—"The Feast," as the Gospel of John 7:37 calls it.

The rabbis say, "He who has not seen Jerusalem during the Feast of Tabernacles does not know what rejoicing means." With a little imagination one can see God's people streaming toward the holy Temple from every town, village, and hamlet in Israel and from distant lands. They bring their tithes and free-will offerings and fulfilled vows. At that time the emptied Temple treasury is opened, to be filled again by the gifts of the faithful, so that the poor and the needy throughout the land might be satisfied.

The Feast of Tabernacles— Commemorative

Apart from its agricultural character, the Feast of Tabernacles also commemorates God's mighty deliverance of His people from Egypt and their forty years of wilderness wandering, when they dwelt in tents and tabernacles.

Israel must never forget that for forty years they were led by the hand of God, nor that they were pilgrims to a better land where God abides.

And so for the last 3,500 years Jews have been observing Succoth, the Feast of Booths, building little tabernacles or booths with walls of plaited branches and thatched roofs, which afford shade by day but permit the stars to gaze down by night upon the Children of Israel as they faithfully fulfill the ancient command: "Ye shall dwell in booths seven days."

The Lulav and the Ethrog

In ancient times there was a controversy between the Sadducees and the Pharisees concerning the booths. The Sadducees held that the "boughs of goodly trees" pertained to the building of the booths. The Pharisees, on the other hand, were of the opinion that the branches were meant to be carried in the

MY, WHAT A BEAUTIFUL LULAV!

hands of the celebrating people. This they called the *lulav.* Eventually a compromise was reached. The booths of branches satisfied the Sadducees. In addition, the people used in their celebration a lulav made of branches of palms, myrtles, and willows, all fastened with a golden thread. These branches of palms, or lulav, were waved in the Temple during certain parts of the service.

Beside the lulav, every Jew came to the Temple holding an *ethrog,* or citrus fruit, symbolic of the fruit of the Promised Land. The booths, lulav, and ethrog are basic symbols of the Feast of Tabernacles.

The Prophetic Character of the Feast of Tabernacles

Numerous sacrifices were offered in the Temple—bullocks, rams, and goats—for a sin-offering. On the first day of the feast thirteen bullocks were offered, twelve the next day, eleven the third, diminishing every day until seven bullocks were offered on the seventh day, making a total of seventy.

The rabbis explain that this number of seventy bullocks was a sacrifice on behalf of the seventy nations of the world, looking toward their conversion to the God of Israel and their gathering under the Shekinah Glory.

The Feast of Tabernacles, like the other feasts of Israel, focuses the attention of God's people both on the past, on what God has done, and on the future, on what God will do. The prophetic message of the Feast of Tabernacles is that there is shelter in the Tabernacle of God under the wings of the Shekinah Glory for the Jew first, and also for the Gentile nations.

Wells of Salvation

Two outstanding features characterized the Temple service during the Feast of Tabernacles: (1) the pouring of water in the Temple, and (2) the brilliant illumination of the Temple.

A specially appointed priest was sent to the Pool of Siloam with a golden pitcher to bring water from the pool. The high priest poured this water into a basin at the foot of the altar. From another pitcher wine was poured into the same basin. These mingled together and flowed through special pipes back to the Brook of Kidron again.

The significance of the pouring of water was twofold. First, it was a symbolic and ritual prayer for abundant rain. Summer was at an end; winter and the rainy season was about to begin. Israel depended upon abundant rain then, as she now does, for her daily bread; hence the prayers for the gates of heaven to open and for abundant rain. Even today in the synagogue much prayer for rain is offered at this time. The pouring of water was a visual interpretation of God's grace in sending rain.

Second, the ritual of water libation went

beyond the mere physical; it was prophetic and messianic in its hope, looking toward the outpouring of the Holy Spirit upon Israel and the believers of all nations under the reign of the Messiah King.

The Day of the Great Hosanna

The ritual of water pouring lasted six days, climaxing on the seventh day, which concluded the Feast of Tabernacles. This day was called *Hoshana Rabba*, the Day of the Great Hosanna. It has a special messianic significance. The pouring of the water from the golden pitcher took place amid the blasting of the trumpets by the priests and the singing of sacred music by the Levites, while the people, waving their lulavs, or palm branches, chanted the Hallel, Psalms 113 –118.

The closing words of Psalm 118 are,

Save now, I beseech thee, O LORD! O LORD, I beseech thee, send now prosperity!

Blessed is he that cometh in the name of the LORD; we have blessed you out of the house of the LORD.

God is the LORD, who hath shown us light; bind the sacrifice with cords, even unto the horns of the altar.

Thou art my God, and I will praise thee; thou art my God, I will exalt thee (Psalm 118:25–28).

From the words "Save now" (in Hebrew,

Hoshana), this day was known as the "Great Hosanna." It was peculiarly messianic in nature, a prayer for speedy salvation through the Messiah. This is why our Savior was greeted on another occasion with the waving of palm branches and the words, "Hosanna to the Son of David," meaning, "Save us, Son of David" (Matthew 21:9). This is important in understanding what happened when the Lord attended the Temple service on the day of the "Great Hosanna."

It was while all this was taking place—the pouring of the water from the Pool of Siloam into the altar basin, the blasting forth of the trumpets by the priests, the singing of the psalms by the Levites, and the prayers of the people, "Save now, I beseech thee, O Lord!" and messianic fervor was at the highest pitch—that the Lord Jesus stood in the Temple crying, "If any man thirst, let him come unto me, and drink. He that believeth on me, as the scripture hath said, out of his heart shall flow rivers of living water" (John 7:37–38). What our Savior said, by implication, was: "I am the answer to your prayers."

The messianic claim of our Savior was clearly understood by all. It must have come like a bolt from the blue. Here was one claiming to be the answer to the fervent hope and prayer of long centuries and many generations. Could he, the carpenter's son of Nazareth, be the long-expected Messiah?

"So there was a division among the people" (John 7:43).

In modern times, on the last day of the Feast of Tabernacles, the Day of the Great Hosanna, the Jews observe the custom of striking the *Arba'ah*, the branches of the willow, three times in an effort to shed all the leaves, which represent sins.

A Messianic Prayer

At this time, special messianic prayers are said. Following is one of the prayers for the day:

A voice heralds, heralds and saith:
Turn unto me and be ye saved, today if ye hear my voice.
Behold the man who sprang forth: Branch is his name—David himself.
Stand up! Be buried in the dust no longer!
Ye who dwell in the dust, wake up and sing.
Glad will be the people when he ruleth;
The name of the ungodly shall perish,
But to His anointed, the Messiah David, He giveth grace.
Grant salvation to the eternal people,
To David and to his seed forever,
The voice heralds and saith.

Upon the completion of this prayer, the leaves of the willow branches are struck three times on the benches of the synagogue. With each falling leaf, a sin falls away from the one who prays. But "The Man who sprang forth, the Messiah David," who alone is able to bring forgiveness of sins, is still unknown in Israel.

Temple Lights and the Light of the World

Another central feature of the Feast of Tabernacles was the illumination of the Temple in Jerusalem. The festive pilgrims came to the Temple bearing lights and torches, while in

AT PRAYER IN JERUSALEM

the Temple itself the golden candlesticks were lighted, transforming the Temple into one brilliant focus of light that illuminated most of Jerusalem and its surroundings. What an eloquent symbol of the Sanctuary of God, that was to be the light of the world!

But the feast ended and the lights were extinguished. Then the next day, our Savior stood and proclaimed, "I am the light of the world" (John 8:12).

Without true knowledge of the rites and symbols of the Feast of Tabernacles, we miss the profound significance of our Lord's pronouncements in the Temple.

Thus, the three aspects of the Feast of Tabernacles stand out boldly: A harvest thanksgiving, a national commemoration of redemption, and faith's leap into the future, when Jehovah shall gather the nations in the Messianic Kingdom of His blessed Son, the Lord Jesus.

With this in mind we understand the vision of Zechariah:

> And it shall come to pass that every one that is left of all the nations which came against Jerusalem shall even go up from year to year to worship the King, the LORD of hosts, and to keep the feast of tabernacles. And it shall be that whoever will not come up of all the families of the earth unto Jerusalem to worship the King, the LORD of hosts, even upon them shall be no rain (14:16–17).

Now we can understand why the punishment for not attending the Feast of Tabernacles was to be the withholding of the rain. The Feast of Tabernacles was preeminently the season when God graciously granted to His people abundant rain. But beyond that, we see even further that the punishment for willful refusal to come and worship the Lord must be the withholding of the outpouring of the blessed Holy Spirit from those who were invited to come but would not.

The Apostle John, looking toward the greater Feast of Ingathering, wrote,

> After this I beheld and, lo, a great multitude, which no man could number, of all nations, and kindreds, and peoples, and tongues, stood before the throne, and before the Lamb, clothed with white robes, and palms in their hands, and cried with a loud voice, saying, Salvation [Hosanna] to our God who sitteth upon the throne, and unto the Lamb (Revelation 7:9–10).

CHAPTER SIX

SIMCHATH TORAH—
THE REJOICING OVER THE LAW

THE Feast of Tabernacles is followed by *Simchath Torah*, which literally means "Rejoicing over the Law."

It arose in the early centuries when the practice of reading the Law of Moses in the synagogues over the period of one year was established. On the Day of Rejoicing over the Law, the reading of the Book of Deuteronomy was completed and Genesis was begun again.

At this time, everyone assembled in the synagogues is called upon to pronounce a blessing over the reading of the Law, and even boys partake. Little children come to the synagogues bearing colorful paper flags with inscriptions extolling the Word of God.

The little flags have lighted candles burning on the flag rod, thrilling the children. In the synagogue the scrolls of the Law, dressed in beautiful velvet mantles of red, scarlet, blue and white, and ornate with golden embroidery and inscriptions, are taken out of the Ark of the Law and lovingly placed in the arms of

"THIS IS THE LAW WHICH MOSES GAVE TO THE CHILDREN OF ISRAEL"

men and even little boys.

These scrolls, "The lively oracles of God," are the most precious possession of Israel. Men lived and died to preserve these for the generations yet unborn. Seven times they march around the synagogue rostrum, singing joyful hymns in honor of the Torah, "Be glad and rejoice with the joy of the Law."

As the solemn procession circles the synagogue auditorium the assembled worshipers kiss the garments of the scrolls, or touch the scrolls with their fingers and then kiss their fingers. This is Israel's token of love and reverence for the Word of God, beautiful in its original conception. But what a sad reflection as we think of Israel's spiritual reality!

There is something tragic about the people rejoicing over their most cherished possession, the Bible, dancing around with their noble, God-given, yet forgotten heritage.

Simchath Torah, the Rejoicing over the Law! Perhaps "The Feast of the Sealed Book" would be a more appropriate name, or "The Feast of a Vision Dimmed and Wisdom Departed."

How well the words of Isaiah describe Israel's relation to the Bible:

> And the vision of all has become unto you like the words of a book that is sealed, which men deliver to one who is learned, saying, Read this, I pray thee; and he saith, I cannot; for it is sealed. And the book is delivered to him who is not learned, saying,

Read this, I pray thee; and he saith, I am not learned.

Wherefore the Lord said, Forasmuch as this people draw near me with their mouth, and with their lips do honor me, but have removed their heart far from me, and their fear toward me is taught by the precept of men; therefore, behold, I will proceed to do a marvelous work among this people . . . for the wisdom of their wise men shall perish, and the understanding of their prudent men shall be hidden (Isaiah 29:11–14).

Israel is yet waiting for her spiritual resurrection, when her eyes will be opened by her Messiah Jesus, the seal broken, and her vision undimmed. Then her wisdom will shine forth for her own healing and for the blessing of the nations. Then it will be Simchath Torah indeed, a true day of rejoicing. The people and the Book will embrace each other, never to be separated.

CHAPTER SEVEN

HANUKKAH—THE FEAST OF DEDICATION AND CHRISTMAS

And it was at Jerusalem the feast of the dedication, and it was winter. And Jesus walked in the temple in Solomon's porch (John 10:22–23).

THIS is the only place in the New Testament where the Feast of Dedication, which the Jews call *Hanukkah*, is mentioned. This festival has been celebrated since the year 164 B.C. and continues to the present time. Hanukkah often coincides with Christmas in that it starts on the 25th day of Kislev, the Jewish month which approximates our December. This identity of dates is more than a mere coincidence. The Feast of Hanukkah and Christmas, the commemoration of the birth of our Lord, are closely related, as we shall see later.

The Story Behind the Feast of Dedication

In the year 169 B.C. Antiochus Epiphanes, the Hellenized ruler of Syria (175–163 B.C.), a vile and godless man, campaigned against Egypt. In spite of his victory there, he was compelled to withdraw from Egypt at the command of powerful Rome. At that time Palestine was under Syrian rule. Returning to Syria, Antiochus vented his wrath upon the hapless Judeans by entering Jerusalem, destroying a large part of the city, and slaughtering men, women, and children. To crown his infamy, he invaded the holy Temple, carrying away the golden altar, the candlesticks, the golden vessels, and other sacred treasures.

To show his contempt for Jehovah, he sacrificed a pig to the Greek god Jupiter. He also sternly forbade the Jews in the Holy Land and abroad to observe their religion, particularly the rite of circumcision, the observance of the Sabbath, and laws pertaining to clean animals.

He commanded that only pigs be sacrificed in the Temple of God. He himself cooked a pig in the Temple and poured its broth on the holy scrolls of the Law and on the altar, thus polluting it sacrilegiously.

Syrian officers and supervisors were dispatched into every city and village of Palestine to enforce the cruel and blasphemous decrees of Antiochus Epiphanes. In terror many of the Jews fled to caves. Others, especially a number of Hellenized priests, complied with the Syrian ruler's commands. But there was a small minority of the faithful who dared defy "Antiochus the Wicked," as he became known in Jewish history.

"Who Is on the Lord's Side?"

One day Apelles, an enforcement officer of Antiochus, arrived in the small township of Modin, three miles north of Jerusalem, and commanded the assembled Jews to sacrifice a hog. Mattathias (Matthew) the Maccabee, head of a priestly family faithful to the Lord and father of five stalwart sons, was enraged by the ungodly decree and killed the first Jew about to comply with the order. Then he and his five sons fell upon Apelles and his group of soldiers and killed them all.

This was the start of an uprising of the Jews against the Syrians, their enemies, and the enemies of their God. Soon after Mattathias died, his son Judas the Maccabee assembled a considerable number of courageous Jews and skillfully led them in battle against the Syrians.

Fired by the courage and devotion of Judas and his four brothers, the once timid and despairing now flocked to the side of their leader. They fought in the mountains and valleys of Judea. They attacked the invaders in guerilla fashion, giving them no respite. As they gained in strength, they ventured to face their enemies in open battle and defeated them.

Finally they drove the Syrians from Jerusalem, together with the disloyal priests who had collaborated with the invaders. After cleansing the holy Temple, they demolished the polluted altar of God. Then on Kislev (December) 25th, 164 B.C., they rededicated the Temple of God, amid great rejoicing, and consecrated a new altar in place of the old.

They did not know, however, what to do with the stones of the old altar—sacred and precious to them but, at the same time, polluted and unfit for the offering of sacrifices. So they decided to heap them together in a corner of the Temple and wait for the coming of Elijah or the Messiah to tell them what to do with these stones.

In light of this, the ancient query of John's disciples, when they asked Jesus, "Art thou he that should come, or do we look for another?" (Matthew 11:3) takes on a special significance. Also the statement of our Savior, "Destroy this temple, and in three days I will raise it up" (John 2:19). They were thinking of a temple made of stones and wood, while the Lord Jesus was referring to Himself, the living Temple of God.

The Miracle of the Cruse of Oil

Hidden in one of the nooks of the Temple the Maccabean Jews found a small jar of consecrated oil, used in former days for the perpetual light in the Temple. The oil was sufficient only for one night, but miraculously the little cruse of oil lasted for eight days, until a new supply could be prepared and consecrated!

In memory of the wonderful redemption from the hands of the wicked enemy and the rededication of the Temple, it was decreed that for eight days eight candles should be lit in every Jewish household, beginning with one on the first day, two on the second, progressively until the eighth day.

The Link

Now we turn to Christmas, or the day when we commemorate our Savior's birth. The Word of God does not indicate the date upon which our Savior was born. Perhaps the Lord, in His wisdom, did not reveal this to us lest we substitute gaudy celebrations and merrymaking—the worship of a day—for the One who is worthy of our worship, love, and service.

It is interesting to note, however, that apparently the early Christians saw a vital link between the Feast of Dedication and the day when Christ was born. On the one hand, a temple made with human hands—on the other, the living Temple of God, which came down from heaven to dwell in our midst. Christ compared Himself to that temple when He said, "Destroy this temple, and in three days I will raise it up" (John 2:19).

And so, since the end of the third century, the 25th of December—which is, according to the Jewish calendar, the 25th of Kislev and the generally accepted date for the day of Hanukkah—has become Christmas.

Of course, this date has never met with universal acceptance, and from the early times of the Church, even to the present day, there have been dissensions and speculations as to which is the day when Christ was born.

The Light of the World

Jesus had declared, following the conclusion of the Feast of Tabernacles, "I am the light of the world; he that followeth me shall not walk in darkness, but shall have the light of life." As with that feast, the Feast of Dedication, too, is always associated with the idea of light overcoming darkness.

Today when the Jews kindle the Hanukkah lights, they are careful to light each candle from the light known as the Servant, a beautiful symbol of Christ, the Servant of God—the Light of the World. He alone is able to kindle in our hearts the light of God. Only in His light can we see light.

Such, briefly, is the relationship between the Feast of Dedication of the Temple, and Christ, the living Temple of God.

The symbol of Hanukkah is a candlestick with nine little candles. The flickering light of nine little candles can mean a great deal in the pitch-darkness of night. But when the sun rises, then candlelight appears pale and insignificant. Thus, to us Christ, the Sun of Righteousness, has dimmed the candles of Hanukkah. We thank God for these small lights, so helpful during the darkness of the past night. But we must now go on to live in the Daylight from on high.

Christmas—the Great Jewish Festival

But even if we know little or nothing of the history of the Feast of Dedication, can any Christian fail to realize that in its very essence, the birth of our Savior is rooted and grounded in the history of Israel? He is God's answer to the promises He made to His people for a Messiah. He is God's answer to the yearnings of Israel for salvation, expressed in a thousand ways in Scripture.

In Christ the hope of Israel became a reality, a reality more glorious, more wonderful than any priest, prophet, or seer ever envisioned.

The people that walked in darkness have seen a great light; they that dwell in the land of the shadow of death, upon them hath the light shined. . . . For unto us a child is born, unto us a son is given, and the government shall be upon his shoulder; and his name shall be called Wonderful, Counselor, The Mighty God, The Everlasting Father, The Prince of Peace. Of the increase of his government and peace there shall be no end, upon the throne of David, and upon his kingdom, to order it, and to establish it with justice and with righteousness from henceforth even forever. The zeal of the LORD of hosts will perform this (Isaiah 9:2, 6–7).

Oh, how we long for the day when both the story of Hanukkah and the story of Christmas will be told in every Jewish home, side by side, and the glory of Christ will dim all past victories and past glories, and He alone will be the King of Glory in every heart. "And so all Israel shall be saved; as it is written, There shall come out of Zion the Deliverer, and shall turn away ungodliness from Jacob" (Romans 11:26).

CHAPTER EIGHT

PURIM—THE FEAST OF ESTHER

He that Keepeth Israel

AMONG the feasts of Israel, *Purim*, also known as the Feast of Esther, holds a favored position. According to some of the rabbis, when Messiah comes, all the feasts will become redundant, but Purim will never cease.

This high esteem for Purim would be puzzling were it not for the fact that it is an expression of faith in the invisible working of an invisible God behind the scenes of human events. The story of Esther is a fitting tribute to the God of an exiled people, without a temple or a priesthood, without a prophet or even a great spiritual leader, who nevertheless are deeply conscious of the divine watchcare on them.

The Book of Esther, so conspicuous by the absence of the name of God, seems to be shouting in its every line and word, "Behold, he who keepeth Israel shall neither slumber nor sleep" (Psalm 121:3).

Purim in Jewish Life

Purim comes on the 14th and 15th days of Adar, the twelfth month of the Biblical year, approximately our March.

Every year during the Feast of Purim, the story of Esther is read with glee in the synagogues. Mordecai's name is cheered, and Haman's is greeted with stomping of the feet, derisive booing, and the grinding sound of special noisemakers. Private and public merriment is the order of the day. Gifts are sent to friends and to the poor in a joyful reenactment of the first Purim, commemorating the deliverance of the Jews from the hands of their enemies, Haman and his henchmen.

As we read the story of Esther, we notice an exquisite fabric of seeming coincidences woven by the invisible but sure hand of God into a pattern that spells deliverance. It has a lesson not only for the Jew but also for all believers: that in the commonplace human events, God moves to accomplish His plans. But it takes the eye of faith to see this.

The setting of the story is ancient Persia at the peak of her power and glory. Some years had passed since 538 B.C., when Cyrus permitted the Jews to return from Babylon to the Holy Land under the leadership of Zerubbabel (Ezra, chapters 1–6).

Those Jews who stayed behind in Babylon chose to live comfortably in dispersion rather than face the hardships of pioneering in their devastated homeland. Among those who decided to remain in exile were Mordecai and Esther. Upon the throne of the Persian Empire, stretching over 127 provinces, was Xerxes (486–465 B.C.), a mighty ruler of nations but a weak character. His decisions were often engineered by self-seeking courtiers and intriguing politicians. The Jewish rabbis were fond of calling Ahasuerus "a fool of a king," probably not without cause.

Yet behind the vacillation and follies of the king, behind intrigues and political maneuvers in the royal court, was God working out His eternal plans. It is fascinating to watch the divine hand behind the "perfectly natural" coincidences, weaving an intricate fabric to shield and protect God's people.

Haman—the Tool of Satan

Haman, the evil spirit of the drama, was a descendant of Amalek, the eternal enemy of Israel, whom God commanded them to destroy utterly (Deuteronomy 25:17-19). It was Saul, the first king of Israel, who disobeyed God and saved Haman's ancestors, thus bringing upon the children of Israel the dire peril of Haman. But, in the artistry of the divine providence, Mordecai, of the same tribe and family as Saul, was chosen to repair the damage. With the annihilation of Haman and his sons, the divine verdict to destroy Amalek was carried out.

But Haman, the prime minister and major-domo of Ahasuerus, did not know these things. This vainglorious politician, obsessed with Jew hatred, was tightening the noose around his own neck without realizing it, for when God would punish someone He first deprives him of his reason.

Haman was a tool of Satan, who from the beginning of the history of the Jews sought to destroy them. Satan knew that out of Abraham's seed would come the One who would bruise his head.

Haman's reaction to Mordecai was perfectly modern. The Jew Mordecai had offended Haman, and so Haman's wrath turned against all the Jews. Historic patterns have a way of repeating themselves.

A Bill of Indictment

When Haman came to Ahasuerus requesting the total destruction of the Jews, he had a ready-made bill of particulars against them. This bill of indictment is worth our analysis:

> And Haman said unto King Ahasuerus, There is a certain people scattered abroad and dispersed among the people in all the provinces of thy kingdom, and their laws are different from all people; neither keep they the king's laws. Therefore, it is not for the king's profit to tolerate them (Esther 3:8).

These accusations are historic because they

have been leveled against the Jews repeatedly throughout their checkered and tragic history.

1. "The Jews are a people scattered abroad and dispersed among all the people." The charge was that the Jews were an alien element in the body of the host nation.

2. "They have different laws." Their religion, customs, and the whole structure of their society and civilization do not fit into the pattern of the host country.

3. "They do not obey the king's laws." This is a charge of disloyalty and lack of patriotism.

4. Summing it all up: "It is not in the king's best interest to tolerate them." They are a burden on the body politic and on the economy of the land, and so they are useless to the king, and the country is better off without them. Solomon the Wise said, "There is no new thing under the sun" (Ecclesiastes 1:9).

A Drastic Solution

"If it please the king, let it be written that they may be destroyed" (Esther 3:9). Haman, like Hitler and countless others, had a ready solution to the Jewish problem: destroy the Jews—total extermination.

Haman was not unaware of the economic value of the Jews to the country. He realized that their absence might hit the king where it hurt. So he offered as a compensation the tidy sum of 10,000 talents of silver (forty to fifty million dollars in our somewhat inflated currency*) "into the hands of those who have charge of the king's treasury." Apparently Haman did not do so badly as a high government official in those remote days in "Shushan, D.C." However, Ahasuerus magnanimously refused to accept the offer and gave Haman the Jews anyway. "Do with them as you like."

How often have the Jews been delivered to the mercy of the merciless! Now the verdict had been pronounced, the trap set. Was there any escape for the hunted?

When Kings and Captains Drink

"The king and Haman sat down to drink; but the city, Shushan, was perplexed" (Esther 3:15). These few words describe in a masterful way the tragedy of the situation. The king and his chief advisor sat down to drink, while Shushan was perplexed.

Woe to a country whose rulers indulge in revelry while their subjects are perplexed. There is something very tragic and ominous about such a state of affairs, and divine retribution cannot be long delayed.

A Remedy That Brings Results

But man's extremity is God's opportunity. The night is darkest just before dawn. Upon hearing the decree, the first reaction of the

---

* Editor's note: This was written in 1954.

Jews was to fast, pray, and repent. What a wholesome example to follow! It is a sure remedy that has never failed to move the heart of God, for it is He who promised, "If my people, who are called by my name, shall humble themselves, and pray, and seek my face, and turn from their wicked ways, then will I hear from heaven, and will forgive their sin, and will heal their land" (2 Chronicles 7:14).

Queen Esther

Meet Esther, First Lady of the great Persian Empire, a humble Jewish maiden elevated to the position of queen by the strange workings of God's design.

Esther and Mordecai show indications of having tried very hard to obliterate their Jewish background. Their very presence in Persia suggests that they had chosen the comforts of that land rather than the hardships of the Holy Land.

Significantly, their names are not Jewish, but rather of Babylonian origin. The name "Mordecai" is believed to be a variant of "Merodach" or "Marduk," the name of the patron deity of Babylon, mentioned in Jeremiah 50:2. "Esther" is strangely reminiscent of the Babylonian goddess "Ishtar" or "Astarte." Their effort to assimilate themselves into their environment has been often repeated in Jewish history. In speech, manner, dress, and by their very names, the Jews have often sought to take on the coloring of the people among whom they live, but in the final analysis, to little avail. Whenever the hour has struck, God has repeatedly sent the Hamans and Hitlers to remind them through blood and tears of their origin and destiny.

There may have been much antagonism against the Jews in the Persian Empire at the time, for Esther's close relative and adoptive father, Mordecai, cautiously advised her not to betray her Jewish nationality to the king or the court. Latent anti-Semitism probably was deep-seated among the people of the Persian Empire, so that Haman found a ready and even eager audience for his Jew hatred. The Hamans and Hitlers of history are only possible where latent hatreds are already pent up in the hearts of the masses. And so Esther guarded the secret of her Jewish descent well—too well. Mordecai had to remind his exalted relative, "Think not with thyself that thou shalt escape in the king's house, more than all the Jews" (Esther 4:13).

Beautiful Esther, queen of the royal household, was afraid to show her true colors while her people were in danger of perishing! What a striking picture of a child of God rejoicing in his own salvation, and at ease while men and women for whom we ought to be burdened and concerned perish.

But when the midnight hour is about to strike, God always sends a deliverer—a Moses in the wilderness; a Samson when the Philistines roam; a Judas Maccabeus when the godless Syrians flood the land and threaten to destroy God's people; a Mordecai and Esther when a sinister Amalekite-Persian seeks to exterminate the "everlasting people."

When the need arises, God has someone specially appointed to come into the kingdom in order to deal with the peril of the hour: "For if thou altogether holdest thy peace at this time, then shall there relief and deliverance arise to the Jews from another place, but thou and thy father's house shall be destroyed. And who knoweth whether thou art come to the kingdom for such a time as this?" (Esther 4:14).

Christian, the Lord has called you into His kingdom for a purpose. He has a special task for you, a precious privilege peculiarly your own. Are you willing to follow His leading, or will the Lord have to replace you with an instrument more yielded to His will? God will bring about His purpose, but you may be passed by.

Esther's determination and devotion are a beautiful testimony for all children of God to follow. "If I perish, I perish." It is only men and women who are willing to lay down their lives in the cause of God whom the Lord can use gloriously. It is not so much gifts and abilities but perfect yieldedness in which the Lord delights.

Shilly-shallying and halfheartedness cannot prosper or be blessed. We remember our Savior's words, "So, then, because thou art lukewarm, and neither cold nor hot, I will spew thee out of my mouth" (Revelation 3:16).

Anti-Semitism, A Blinding Obsession

Haman basked in the honors bestowed upon him by his lord and master, Ahasuerus. He related to his wife and friends the dignities already bestowed upon him and gleefully anticipated honors yet to come. But the fly in Haman's ointment was Mordecai, the Jew, the obstinate Jew with the unbending knee. Oh, if only he could get rid of Mordecai, his bliss would be unmarred. And Mordecai the Jew became Haman's obsession—an obsession not unlike that among many otherwise reasonable and intelligent people. When you speak to them they are rational, as long as you do not touch the subject of the Jew. But mention the Jews and they see red. The Jews, in their imagination, are behind everything. All their own personal problems and frustrations, all international complexities and human woes, all that ever went wrong is due to the Jews—the serpent in the fool's paradise.

A Bit of Divine Irony

There is a bit of divine irony in the story of Haman. He who schemes and plans the destruction of the Jews invokes divine wrath against himself. Haman, in his blindness, and in pursuit of his own aggrandizement, unknowingly sets the stage for Mordecai's promotion and his own humiliation and final destruction. He seeks to hang Mordecai, but the very gallows that he erects for Mordecai is destined to destroy its designer.

Haman was only one in the long procession of men whom God has raised up to confirm the truth of His Word: "No weapon that is formed against thee [the Jews] shall prosper" (Isaiah 54:17).

". . . and Hate Thine Enemies"

The Book of Esther has often been the pretext for severe criticism even among Christians (Luther, for example). The Jews, the critics have said, are revengeful and unforgiving. In this matter we would like to make a few basic observations.

First, let us remember that we are dealing with a people in a pre-Christian dispensation. The gospel of forgiveness and love has not been made known to them. It is a dispensation of retribution, and laws of severe justice prevail—a life for a life and an eye for an eye. A man who does not take two eyes for one eye is considered righteous. It was our Savior Himself who reminded His listeners, "Ye have heard that it hath been said, Thou shalt love thy neighbor, and hate thine enemy" (Matthew 5:43).

Such was the spirit of the time in which the drama of Mordecai and Esther was enacted. It is only in the light of the times and the revelation given to the people that we may judge them.

The natural man hates his enemies, and when he loves his friends this is considered to be a great virtue. Only our Savior prayed on the cross to which His enemies nailed Him, "Father, forgive them; for they know not what they do" (Luke 23:34).

Another point to be considered is that Esther asked for the right of self-defense for her people. This was granted to them, and when the appointed hour for their destruction came, they had the privilege and encouragement of the king to stand in their own defense. Of this they availed themselves, not unwillingly. Yet they were especially careful not to take any spoil from their defeated enemies, lest the stigma of robbery attach itself to them.

And So We Have Purim

In commemoration of that great deliverance, Mordecai and Esther instituted the Feast of Purim, which means "lots." "Wherefore, they called these days Purim after the name of Pur" (Esther 9:26). The idolatrous and superstitious Haman decided to find out which would be the most propitious day to destroy the Jews and so he cast lots. The lot fell upon the 13th day of Adar, the twelfth month in God's calendar.

But the day appointed for the defeat and destruction of the Jews was turned into their day of deliverance. In the final analysis, their victory is the victory of God over Satan, the victory of prayer, fasting, and faith over pagan wrath and blind hatred. It is the victory of the providence and loving-kindness of Jehovah, who neither slumbers nor sleeps.

Purim, like the preceding Feast of Hanukkah, is a link in the chain of preservation and redemption which God Himself has forged for His people. Purim is a signpost on the road of salvation, ascending from physical deliverance to the perfect redemption which only the Lord Jesus Christ can give to those who accept His sacrifice upon the cross of Calvary.

The partial, imperfect, physical deliverance which God wrought through Mordecai points to Christ, who is able to save to the uttermost.

"Wherefore, the law was our schoolmaster to bring us unto Christ" (Galatians 3:24).

CHAPTER NINE

SABBATH THE QUEEN

The sun has disappeared beyond the trees.
Let us go forth to greet Sabbath the Queen.
Behold she comes, the holy and blest,
And with her the angels of peace and rest.
Come in, come in, Blessed Queen,
Peace be unto you too, you angels of peace.

Israel's Exclusive Heritage

FOR generations untold, the Sabbath has been to the Jew the Queen and Bride of the soul, a God-appointed day of rest and worship.

The Sabbath is deeply imbedded in the heart of Judaism, a pivotal point of Jewish life. Sabbath and circumcision are the two distinguishing marks of Judaism. No one can be thought of as a truly religious Jew, in the rabbinical sense, unless he observes both.

"Sabbath" means "rest." It is preeminently and distinctly a Jewish holiday, given by God to the Children of Israel through His servant Moses on the Mount of Sinai.

And the LORD spoke unto Moses, saying, Speak thou also unto the children of Israel, saying, Verily my sabbaths ye shall keep; for it is a sign between me and you throughout your generations, that ye may know that I am the LORD who doth sanctify you. Ye shall keep the sabbath therefore; for it is holy unto you: every one that defileth it shall surely be put to death; for whosoever doeth any work therein, that soul shall be cut off from among his people (Exodus 31:12–14).

The Sabbath is exclusively Israel's heritage, given under the Law to the people of the Law. The observance of the Sabbath, as originally ordained by God, presupposes the existence of a holy Temple, a God-appointed priesthood, and a sacrificial system.

And on the sabbath day, two lambs of the first year without spot, and two tenth parts of flour for a meal offering, mixed with oil, and the drink offering thereof; this is the burnt offering of every sabbath, besides the continual burnt offering, and its drink offering (Numbers 28:9–10).

The Sabbath Observed in Breach Only

As things stand today, a Jew cannot observe the Sabbath in its scriptural setting, because the essential conditions for such observances are absent. What the Jews of today try to observe is the rabbinical version of the Sabbath. But this much-changed Sabbath is even more impossible to strictly observe, for the following reasons:

The vast majority of Jews simply are unfamiliar with the intricate system of rabbinical law, without the knowledge of which it is impossible to keep the Sabbath.

The rabbis always sought to make the breaking of the Torah (the Law) as difficult as possible. To achieve it, they built up what they called a "Fence around the Law." They made injunctions and regulations prohibiting things that God Himself never forbade. It is as if the United States Congress, in an effort to keep inviolate the gold of Fort Knox, would forbid anyone even to approach the state boundaries of Kentucky. Anyone setting foot on the soil of Kentucky would be considered as if he actually broke in and robbed the gold of Fort Knox.

The recorded teachings of these ancient rabbis (approximately second to fifth century A.D.) are know as the Talmud. The Talmud is a collection of Scripture commentaries and folklore—a treasury of legendary and historical material, including the record of legal discussions pertaining to all aspects of Jewish life. One of its treatises is called "Sabbath" and deals with matters related to the observance of the Sabbath.

1521 Sabbath Rules

In the treatise "Sabbath" the rabbis established 39 categories of activities that may not be performed on the Sabbath. These categories of forbidden activities are called *Aboth*, or "Fathers." In turn, these main 39 categories are subdivided into 39 classes which are called *Toledoth*, or "Offspring," making a total of 39 x 39, or 1521 Sabbath rules.

The most simple and trivial matter of daily occurrence is the subject of involved disputes and ingenious rabbinical legislation. We venture to say that not one Jew in a thousand knows them all, even approximately.

The preparation of food for the Sabbath constitutes a vast and complicated subject of

CHILDREN KINDLING SABBATH LIGHTS

discussion and rabbinical ingenuity. All travel on the Sabbath, even to a synagogue service, is forbidden. The kindling of fire, and even the turning on or off of electric lights, is prohibited. Also writing of any kind is forbidden, etc., etc.

Questions such as these are discussed at great length: How far may a man walk on the Sabbath Day? What may he carry on the Sabbath Day without breaking the law of not bearing burdens? What is a burden? Is the carrying of a handkerchief a burden? The answer is *yes*, if it is in the pocket; but *no*, if it is tied around the neck and thus used as a piece of apparel.

The Genius of Hairsplitting

The question of whether an egg laid on the Sabbath Day is fit for consumption constitutes the subject of a very learned and involved discussion. These and thousands of other questions are most seriously and learnedly discussed by great rabbis, whom men call "sages," or "wise men."

These "wise men" erected fences and hedges around the Law and then turned around and showed how they might be circumvented. In this way, they created a veritable system of prohibitions and evasions.

The rabbis themselves seem to have been aware of the flimsy structure of their injunctions and prohibitions. One of them rightly observed: "Some of the laws of the Sabbath are like mountains suspended on a hair" (Chagigah 10a).

Here we have a bewildering example of where man's wisdom leads without the inspiration of the Holy Spirit. Man-made "religion" is not necessarily a blessing.

> For it is written, I will destroy the wisdom of the wise, and will bring to nothing the understanding of the prudent. . . . For after that, in the wisdom of God, the world by wisdom knew not God, it pleased God by the foolishness of preaching to save them that believe (1 Corinthians 1:19, 21).

Human wisdom unaided by the Holy Spirit invariably leads to lifeless sterility—busy windmills grinding no grain and providing no bread whereby man can live.

We must not for a moment single out for condemnation the rabbis, those "great masters of little things." Parallel developments have taken place in other religions as well, both pagan and so-called "Christian." For example, the scholastic theology of the Medieval Church has no occasion to envy the learned rabbis. Its theologians, too, created what might be called a "Christian Talmud."

A disputation concerning how many angels can dance on the head of a pin (by a learned monk) is by no means more inspiring than the discussion by some learned rabbi as to whether it is permissible on the Sabbath to wipe the mud off one's shoes.

The average Jew of today, absorbed in the cares of life, has neither the time nor the inclination to study these things. And even if he did, the very effort to observe these laws, especially under modern conditions, would constitute a burden impossible to fulfill. Nevertheless, in spite of all that, devout Jews have tried to observe the Sabbath and have done it with great joy.

Seven Is Sacred

Seven is a hallowed number in Scripture. The Lord created the world in six days and sanctified the seventh day as a day of rest—Sabbath.

As the seventh day is dedicated to God, so is the seventh month. It is the month of holy assemblies and seasons.

The New Year of the Jews falls on the first day of the seventh month, a day when God commanded a holy convocation, a day of rest and repentance, a day of sounding of the ram's horn.

The tenth day of the seventh month is the solemn Day of Atonement. The fifteenth day of the seventh month is the beginning of the eight-day Feast of Tabernacles.

The seventh year is also sacred unto God, a Sabbatical year:

Six years thou shalt sow thy field, and six years thou shalt prune thy vineyard, and gather in the fruit thereof; but in the seventh year shall be a sabbath of rest unto the land, a sabbath for the LORD: thou shalt neither sow thy field, nor prune thy vineyard (Leviticus 25:3–4).

The Year of Jubilee

When seven Sabbatical years had been completed, the fiftieth year was a Year of Jubilee.

And thou shalt number seven sabbaths of years unto thee, seven times seven years; and the space of the seven sabbaths of years shall be unto thee forty and nine

A KNOTTY POINT

years. Then shalt thou cause the trumpet of the jubilee to sound on the tenth day of the seventh month, in the day of atonement shall ye make the trumpet sound throughout all your land.

And ye shall hallow the fiftieth year, and proclaim liberty throughout all the land unto all the inhabitants thereof: it shall be a jubilee unto you; and ye shall return every man unto his possession, and ye shall return every man unto his family. . . . In the year of this jubilee ye shall return every man unto his possession (Leviticus 25: 8–10, 13).

The Year of Jubilee is one of the most wonderful provisions God made for His people, reflecting His great mercy and love. In the Year of Jubilee the man who had become poor had the opportunity to receive back his possessions lost through poverty, after making fair arrangements with the man who had come into possession of the property belonging to the impoverished brother.

If thy brother hath become poor, and hath sold away some of his possession, and if any of his kin come to redeem it, then shall he redeem that which his brother sold (Leviticus 25:25).

All Hebrew servants were also to be set free. An Israelite was to be no man's bondservant, but God's.

Sabbath Today

With the continuous erosion of religious life, the Sabbath observance has become more and more neglected. Some do not care, and others are simply forced by economic conditions to work or trade on the Sabbath just as on any other day. Some Reformed Jews observe Sunday as their day of rest, in keeping with the social pattern of life in the West. But a considerable number of Jews still try to observe the Sabbath according to rabbinical injunctions.

Since we have pointed out some rabbinical foibles, it is only fair that we also mention something that is good and wholesome in their teaching. Much of what the rabbis thought still reflected the spirit of the Word of God, its righteousness and its mercy. Since the Sabbath Day is to be a day of rejoicing, they encourage the providing of good things, not only for their own families but also for the poor and the stranger:

> And when he [the Jew] eats and drinks, he is bound to feed the stranger, the orphan, and the widow, with the poor. But he that bolts the doors of his house, and eats and drinks with his children and his wife, but does not furnish meat and drink to the poor and afflicted, is not to be regarded as having fulfilled the commandment; on the contrary, his joy is that of a glutton, and of

such persons it is said, "Their sacrifices shall be unto them as the bread of mourners; all that eat thereof shall be polluted; for their bread for their soul shall not come into the house of the Lord"—Hosea 9:4 (Arbah Turim 529).

The Beauty of Holiness

The Sabbath, even when marred by human distortion, still casts a glow on the family life of the observant Jew. Man has not been able to obliterate altogether some of the heavenly beauty that the Lord has instilled into the Sabbath Day, which He has sanctified and made holy.

Like all other religious holidays, the Sabbath begins at sunset of the preceding day, that is, on Friday evening. There is a service in the synagogue consisting of special prayers of welcome for the Sabbath, the Bride and Queen. The home is festively decorated, the tables decked, candles lit, and a special holiday supper is prepared for the family after they return home from the synagogue. A cup of wine is blessed and distributed among the members of the family. This is known as *Kiddush*, which means "sanctification."

After the supper, a prayer of thanksgiving for the food is said, and hymns of praise in honor of the Sabbath are chanted.

Crown of days, above all blest,
The Rock of Ages chose thee for His rest.

Six days are for toil created
But the seventh God has consecrated.
Do no labor! Thus He bade us.
In six days a world He made us.
Crown of days, above all blest,
The Rock of Ages chose thee for His rest.

Some of the hymns have definite Messianic overtones, such as the following:

Elijah the Prophet,
Elijah the Tishbite,
Elijah the Gileadite,
Come quickly to us
And bring the Messiah, the Son of David.

The devotion through the ages of the Jew to the Sabbath has been something beautiful

A SABBATH AFTERNOON IN TEL AVIV

and heroic. It has set them apart from the Gentile world and has been a testimony and challenge not only to the pagans but to Christians as well. Like circumcision, the Sabbath has helped to preserve the identity of the Jews and the very life of the Jewish people.

One of the Jewish thinkers, Achad Ha-am, truly observed: "Even more than the Jews have kept the Sabbath, has the Sabbath kept the Jews."

But what about the Christian? Is he under obligation to keep the Sabbath? Should he keep Sunday as the Lord's Day or observe the Sabbath of the Jews? How should he keep it? Is Sunday worship a "papal" invention, as some maintain?

CHAPTER TEN

SABBATH OR
THE LORD'S DAY—WHICH?

T HE subject of Sabbath versus Sunday observance presents one of the most heated
controversies not only between Synagogue
and Church, but within the Church itself,
causing considerable confusion even among
believers. We will attempt to turn some light
on the subject from the Word of God and the
earliest records of the Christian Church.

"Why do thy disciples not keep the Sabbath?" was one of the chief reproaches of the
Jewish elders and the Pharisees against our
Lord and His disciples. Yet our Lord, in de-
fending the deeds of love and healing which
He performed on the Sabbath Day and the
plucking of the ears of grain by His hungry
disciples, did not reject the observance of the
Sabbath as such. What He did repudiate was
the heavy burdens that the rabbis imposed
upon the people, man-made impositions, not
based on the authority of the Word of God. He
who was the Son of God was by virtue of His
Messiahship also the Lord of the Sabbath.

"For the Son of Man is Lord even of the sabbath day" (Matthew 12:8).

But as long as our Savior was in the flesh He lived under the law into which He was born. The crucified and risen Savior fulfilled the whole purpose of the law.

"But, when the fullness of the time was come, God sent forth his Son, made of a woman, made under the law, to redeem them that were under the law, that we might receive the adoption of sons" (Galatians 4:4–5).

The law came to show men what God required of them, but Christ came to bring the grace that enables them to do the will of God.

The law was given to the Jews as a people, and the Sabbath together with circumcision were the foremost signs of God's covenant with Israel. The law code of Moses was not intended for the Gentiles.

The early Christian Church, into which many Gentile believers had come, was beset by strife and problems centering around the observance or nonobservance of the ceremonial and ritual law. Even today, the Church is still vexed by some of these problems. As of old, so even now some people insist on keeping the Sabbath. Paul warned the believers against such:

Ye are circumcised with the circumcision made without hands, in putting off the body of the sins of the flesh by the circumcision of Christ. . . . Let no man, therefore, judge you in food, or in drink, or in respect of a feast day, or of the new moon, or of a sabbath day, which are a shadow of things to come; but the body is of Christ (Colossians 2:11, 16–17).

The Apostle Paul clearly indicated that the Sabbath does not apply to the Christian but is only for the Jew who lived under the dispensation of the law of Moses. In the previous chapter it was pointed out that even the Jew finds it impossible to keep the Sabbath in all its stringency. How much less can the Gentile hope to keep it effectively? The law only serves to emphasize our helplessness in the face of God's command and squarely throws us upon the mercy and grace of God.

Significantly the Jewish rabbis themselves have always thought of the Sabbath as being exclusively the privilege of Israel, basing this on Exodus 31:12–17. Because of this, they have resented any Gentile attempt to keep the Sabbath or any other part of the law code without complete submission to the law in its entirety. The following words give expression to their sentiments:

A Gentile who employs himself in the law is guilty of death. Thus a Gentile who keeps a Sabbath, though it be on one of the weekdays, if he make it to himself as a Sabbath, he is guilty of death. Either let a Gentile become a proselyte of righteousness [a convert to Judaism] and take upon him the whole law: or let him remain in his own law, and neither add nor diminish. But if he employs himself in the law, or keeps a Sabbath, or makes any innovation, he is to be beaten and punished, and informed that he for this is guilty of death; but he is not to be killed (Hilchoth Melachim 10:9).

The Difference Between the Sabbath and the Lord's Day

There are basic differences between the Sabbath of the Jew and the Lord's Day that we need to always bear in mind:

1. The Sabbath, or the seventh day of the week, commemorates a completed physical creation (Genesis 2:1–3).

The first day of the week is the day of resurrection and signifies a completed redemption (Matthew 28:1–6).

2. The Sabbath is a covenant sign between God and His people Israel: "Speak thou also unto the children of Israel, saying, Verily my sabbaths ye shall keep; for it is a sign between me and you throughout your generations, that ye may know that I am the LORD who doth sanctify you" (Exodus 31:13).

The first day of the week signifies the fellowship between the Church and her Lord: "And upon the first day of the week, when the disciples came together to break bread, Paul preached unto them, ready to depart on the next day" (Acts 20:7).

3. The Sabbath observance was commanded by the law. The punishment for noncompliance was death: "Ye shall keep the sabbath therefore; for it is holy unto you: every one that defileth it shall surely be put to death; for whosoever doeth any work therein, that soul shall be cut off from among his people" (Exodus 31:14).

The Lord's Day is a day of voluntary, spontaneous worship without any commandment—a day of witness and labor for the Lord.

4. The Sabbath is an essential part of the covenant of works. The Lord's Day is representative of the covenant of grace.

5. The Sabbath is the crowning day of the week and rewards man for his toil. The Lord's Day emphasizes what God has done for man through His only begotten Son.

It is significant that all of the commandments of the Decalogue are mentioned in one form or another throughout the New Testament as a moral code that applies to the believer, whether he be Jew or Gentile. But there is one exception, the fourth commandment, the keeping of the Sabbath, which is commanded nowhere in the New Testament.

The Parting Was Painful

Jewish believers in Christ were in a dilemma from the very beginning. Eventually it forced them out of the synagogue into a fellowship that was distinctly Christian, the *ecclesia*.

The dilemma of the Jewish Christians was this: By the ties of blood and by the affection of their heart, they felt themselves to be an integral part of Israel. They differed, however, from their unbelieving brethren by their faith in the Lord, the Messiah Jesus, to whom they owed supreme allegiance. For some time after the resurrection, the Jewish believers still attended the Temple worship in Jerusalem: "And they, continuing daily with one accord in the temple, and breaking bread from house to house . . ." (Acts 2:46).

Nevertheless, the separation between believers and unbelievers was soon forced upon the Jewish Christians by violence and persecution. The first martyr for the faith was Stephen. Active persecution of Jewish believers, vilification of the person of the Lord Jesus, and changes in the liturgy to include direct or implicit denunciation of the believers in the Messiah Jesus drove the Jewish Christians out of the Temple and the synagogue.

To the daily prayers of the synagogue was added the *Birkath-Hamminim*, "The Blessing of the Sectarians," which was in reality a malediction. Here is the wording of this strange "blessing," as in the original Hebrew version:

And for the Apostates let there be no

hope, and the dominion of arrogance [probably Rome—Editor's note] may it be speedily uprooted in our days. Let the Nazarenes [Jewish Christians] and the Sectarians perish as in a moment. May they be blotted out from the Book of Life and with the Righteous Ones may they not be inscribed. Blessed art thou, Jehovah, who humblest the arrogant.

Even today this prayer, in a considerably changed form, is used in the synagogue. But the word "Apostates" has been changed to "Slanderers," and the direct reference to the

Upper Jordan in Galilee

Nazarenes and the Sectarians is omitted.

Obviously a Jewish Christian could not remain in the synagogue where his Lord was slandered and he himself was made the subject of cursing.

If the gospel was not to be confined to the narrow territorial and spiritual boundaries of Judea, the breach had to come, so that the gospel of salvation might have free course, not only among the Jews, but also among the nations. So God allowed persecution: "As for Saul, he made havoc of the church, entering into every house and, haling men and women, committed them to prison. Therefore, they that were scattered abroad went everywhere preaching the word" (Acts 8:3–4).

The final breach took place in the times of the false Messiah, Bar Kochba, who fought against the Romans and died in battle in A.D. 135. The Jewish believers could not endorse his claims nor support his warfare. Believers had to leave Jerusalem and eventually Palestine. Henceforth, the Church and the Synagogue went their separate paths. The daughter was forcibly weaned from her mother.

The First Christians and the Sabbath Question

At first Jewish believers apparently continued for some time in the voluntary observance of the Sabbath, not because they felt their salvation rested upon this but, rather, out of regard for the sensibilities of their own people. At the same time, they felt the inner need to assemble themselves on the day of our Savior's triumph—His resurrection—to break bread and remember His death and coming again. Prayers were offered and the Word preached (Acts 20).

After the early Jewish Church was scattered abroad and the majority of new believers were coming from among the Gentiles, the Sabbath observance was falling into disuse. The Church was now faced with a fierce struggle between two incompatible groups. One represented the Judaizing element of the Church, who believed that in order for a Gentile to become a Christian he must first become a Jew and conform to all the law of Moses. Opposed to this group was the main fellowship of the Christian Church, those who believed that Gentile believers were under no such obligation to the law. The New Testament, especially in the Acts of the Apostles and Paul's epistles to the Galatians and the Colossians, vividly depicts this struggle.

The matter came to a head at the first Christian Synod in Jerusalem (Acts 15). Our Lord's brother James, the first bishop of Jerusalem, presided (not St. Peter—the alleged first pope) and gave the following ruling:

Forasmuch as we have heard that certain who went out from us have troubled you with words, subverting your souls, saying,

Ye must be circumcised, and keep the law, to whom we gave no such commandment, it seemed good unto us, being assembled with one accord. . . . For it seemed good to the Holy Spirit, and to us, to lay upon you no greater burden than these necessary things: that ye abstain from things offered to idols, and from blood, and from things strangled, and from fornication; from which, if ye keep yourselves, ye shall do well. Fare ye well (Acts 15:24–25, 28–29).

The imposition of the Sabbath upon the Gentile believers is conspicuous by its absence—not a word about it.

After that first synod in Jerusalem, Paul devoted all his energy in defense of the *gospel of grace* against all those who would impose the legal system of Moses as a necessity for Gentile believers. His heart agonized when he saw the confusion and deadening effects of the Judaizing teachings upon the Gentile converts. The following passages give us a glimpse into Paul's heart:

O foolish Galatians, who hath bewitched you, that ye should not obey the truth, before whose eyes Jesus Christ hath been openly set forth, crucified among you? This only would I learn of you, Received ye the Spirit by the works of the law, or by the hearing of faith? . . . For as many as are of the works of the law are under the curse;

for it is written, Cursed is everyone that continueth not in all things which are written in the book of the law, to do them. But that no man is justified by the law in the sight of God, it is evident; for, The just shall live by faith. And the law is not of faith. . . . For in Christ Jesus neither circumcision availeth anything, nor uncircumcision, but a new creature (Galatians 3:1–2, 10–12; 6:15).

For Paul, to cling to the Sabbath was to cling to the beggarly elements—to exchange the glorious reality of Christ for the mere shadow that the law code of Moses represents.

The main body of the Church, consisting of both Jews and Gentiles, began very early to observe the first day of the week as "The Lord's Day." There were, however, some Jews who persisted in the observance of the Sabbath as well as other rites of the ceremonial law. They had no fellowship with the other Christians who did not observe the law.

These Judaizing Hebrew believers, called Nazarenes and Ebionites, were cut off from the main flow of Christian life and fellowship within the Church and in time they vanished from the horizon. They were eventually swallowed up by Judaism or Gnosticism.

The historical record of the early Christians indicates clearly that the first day became the Christian day of worship—the Lord's Day: "And upon the first day of the week, when the disciples came together to break bread, Paul preached unto them, ready to depart on the next day, and continued his speech until midnight" (Acts 20:7).

Barnabas, one of the Apostolic Fathers of the first century A.D., wrote: "We keep the Lord's Day with joyfulness, the day on which Jesus rose from the dead."

The "Didache of the Apostles," one of the earliest Christian documents (also of the first century), which contained the teachings of the apostles, states: "On the Lord's own day gather yourselves together and break bread and give thanks."

Ignatius, Bishop of Antioch, in the year A.D. 110, said: "Those who walked in the ancient practices attain unto newness of hope, no longer observing sabbaths, but fashioning their lives after the Lord's Day, on which our life also rose through Him, that we may be found disciples of Jesus Christ, our only teacher."

Justin Martyr, in the year A.D. 135, said: "Sunday is the day on which we all hold common assembly, because it is the *first* day on which God, having wrought a change in the darkness and matter, made the world; and Jesus Christ our Savior on the same day rose from the dead. And on the day called Sunday all who live in cities or in the country gather together to one place and the memoirs of the apostles or the writings of the prophets are read as long as time permits."

These are just a few of the historic documents of the early Church relating to the subject.

To maintain, as some do, that the observance of the first day of the week as the Lord's Day was instituted by the popes or by Constantine the Great in the fourth century is to betray a basic ignorance of New Testament facts and to fly in the face of the recorded history of the Christian Church. In reality, Constantine the Great (so-called), upon accepting Christianity, enacted in A.D. 321 the first "Sunday Law," making the Sunday observance obligatory for the Roman Empire. But that had been the practice of Christians since the days of the apostles.

The Sabbath-Versus-Sunday Issue

The Jews of the Western world often find themselves in a peculiar predicament. Their Gentile neighbors work on the Sabbath and take Sunday off for worship (if believers) or pleasure (if unbelievers).

The Jew, closely integrated with the economic and social pattern of life, is often forced to work on the Sabbath and to relax on Sunday. If he is to worship at all, he may have to do it on Sunday. It has therefore become a practice, at least among some Reformed Jews, to hold "Sabbath" services on Sunday.

Conversely, Jewish Christians in Israel are faced with the same problem in reverse—observing "Sunday" on Saturday.

In the new State of Israel the believers live in a Jewish economy. The Sabbath is the legal day of rest; Sunday is a work day like every other day. Most believers are, therefore, unable to gather together on Sunday and consequently have to worship the Lord, attend services, and pray on the Sabbath. To insist that the Hebrew Christian should not work on Sunday would mean jeopardizing his already precarious existence. Shall we judge him for that?

The position of the Israeli Christian today closely parallels that of his believing ancestors in the early Church. We could not do better than follow the Apostle Paul, who gave us very clear guidance in this matter:

> One man esteemeth one day above another; another esteemeth every day alike. Let every man be fully persuaded in his own mind. He that regardeth the day, regardeth it unto the Lord; and he that regardeth not the day, to the Lord he doth not regard it. He that eateth, eateth to the Lord; for he giveth God thanks; and he that eateth not, to the Lord he eateth not, and giveth God thanks. For none of us liveth to himself, and no man dieth to himself (Rom. 14:5–7).

The keeping of the Lord's Day, dedicated to divine worship and witness, is a godly, wholesome, and altogether commendable practice, refreshing for the body and quickening to the spirit. Furthermore, it is based on the example and practice of the first Christians, according to scriptural and post-scriptural testimony. Yet our salvation does not rest upon the observance of any particular day, be it Saturday or Sunday. The point we must remember in all these matters is that our salvation rests entirely and uncompromisingly on the finished work of Calvary. Salvation is based on what the Lord has done and not on what we do. We can neither add nor subtract from it, but must accept it through faith.

In the State of Israel, the Jewish believer may wish, out of loyalty to his people, to observe the Sabbath, to practice circumcision, or to refuse to eat pork. As long as he docs not makc this a qucstion of salvation, it matters little. Said the Apostle Paul, "Unto the Jews I became as a Jew, that I might gain the Jews" (1 Corinthians 9:20).

A Rest to the People of God

The Lord's Day is a day of spiritual rest—not a day of idleness, or of man-enforced prohibitions, but a day when "peace like a river" floods the soul.

This kind of Sabbath is unknown to the Jew, but it is the blessed experience and heritage of the child of God who has found rest and peace in the Messiah of the Jews, the Lord Jesus Christ.

There remaineth, therefore, a rest [a Sabbath] to the people of God. For he that is entered into his rest, he also hath ceased from his own works, as God did from his. Let us labor, therefore, to enter into that rest, lest any man fall after the same example of unbelief (Hebrews 4:9–11).

The Liberty Wherewith Christ Has Made Us Free

Those of us who have been raised under the law know the deadening effect of the law: "The letter killeth, but the Spirit giveth life" (2 Corinthians 3:6). How pathetic and misguided is the Christian who would induce anyone, Jew or Gentile, who has known "the liberty with which Christ hath made us free" (Galatians 5:1) to take upon himself again the burden of the law. With the Apostle Paul, we feel like saying, "O foolish Galatians, who hath bewitched you?"

Years ago in Poland when I was a little Jewish boy of about five years, I remember the *Melamed*, the teacher of religion, as he led little recalcitrant boys by the hand to *Cheder*, the religious school of instruction. There the children were taught the Hebrew alphabet and the rudiments of the Scriptures. The Apostle Paul had a very similar picture in mind when he said, "Wherefore, the law was our schoolmaster to bring us unto Christ, that we might be justified by faith" (Galatians 3:24). The word for schoolmaster in Greek is *paidagogos*, literally, "the one who leads the boy."

The law code of Moses has led us by the hand to Christ.

Only one who has lived under law and has come to know the liberating power of grace, may sing,

Free from the law, O happy condition!
Jesus hath bled, and there is remission;
Cursed by the law and bruised by the fall,
Christ hath redeemed us once for all.

This book was produced by the Christian Literature Crusade. We hope it has been helpful to you in living the Christian life. CLC is a literature mission with ministry in over 45 countries worldwide. If you would like to know more about us, or are interested in opportunities to serve with a faith mission, we invite you to write to:

Christian Literature Crusade
P.O.Box 1449
Fort Washington, PA 19034